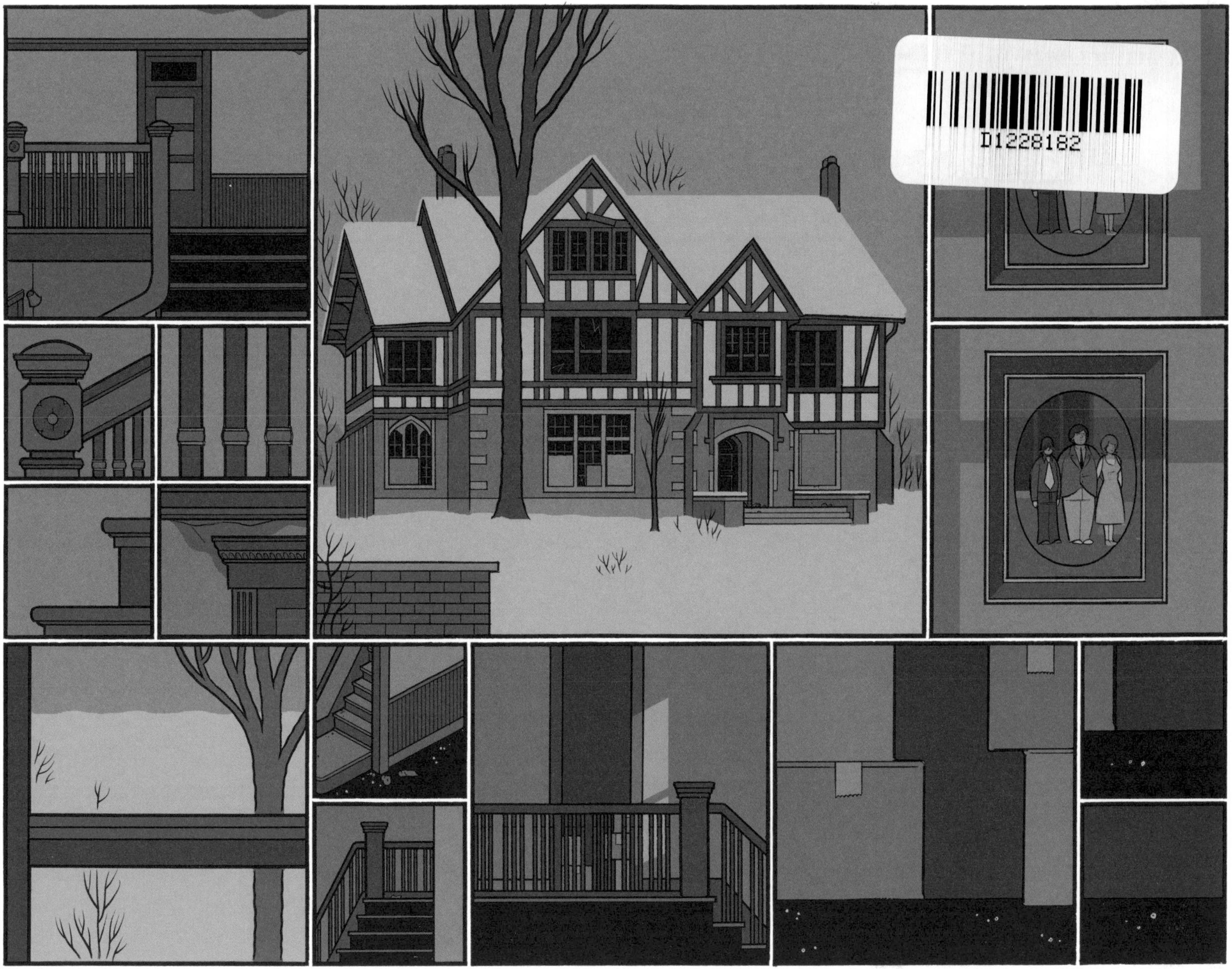

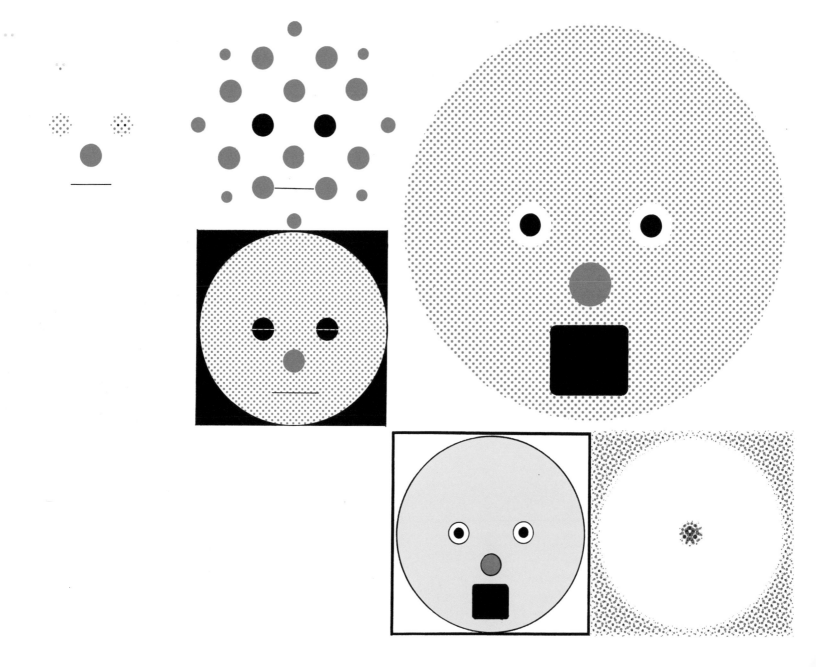

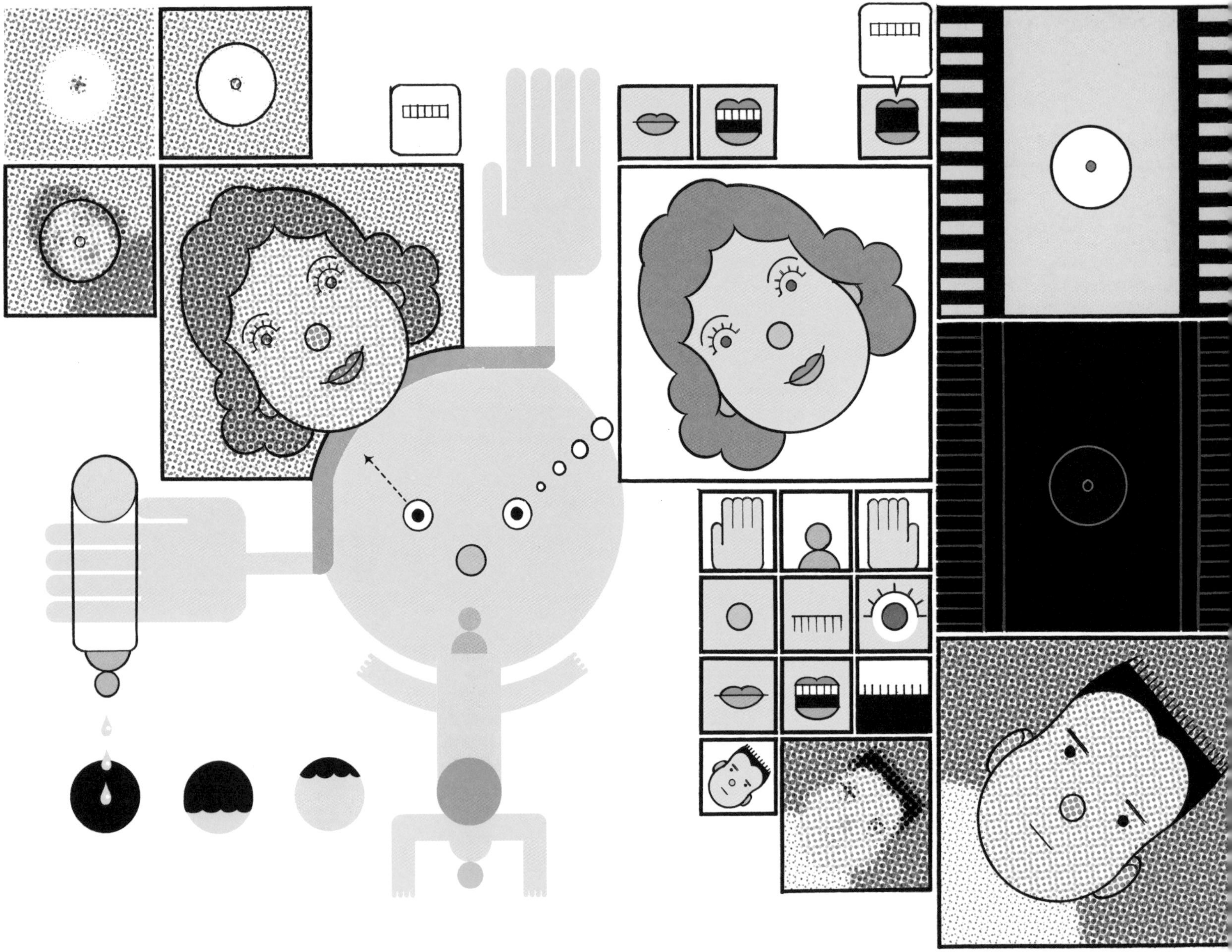

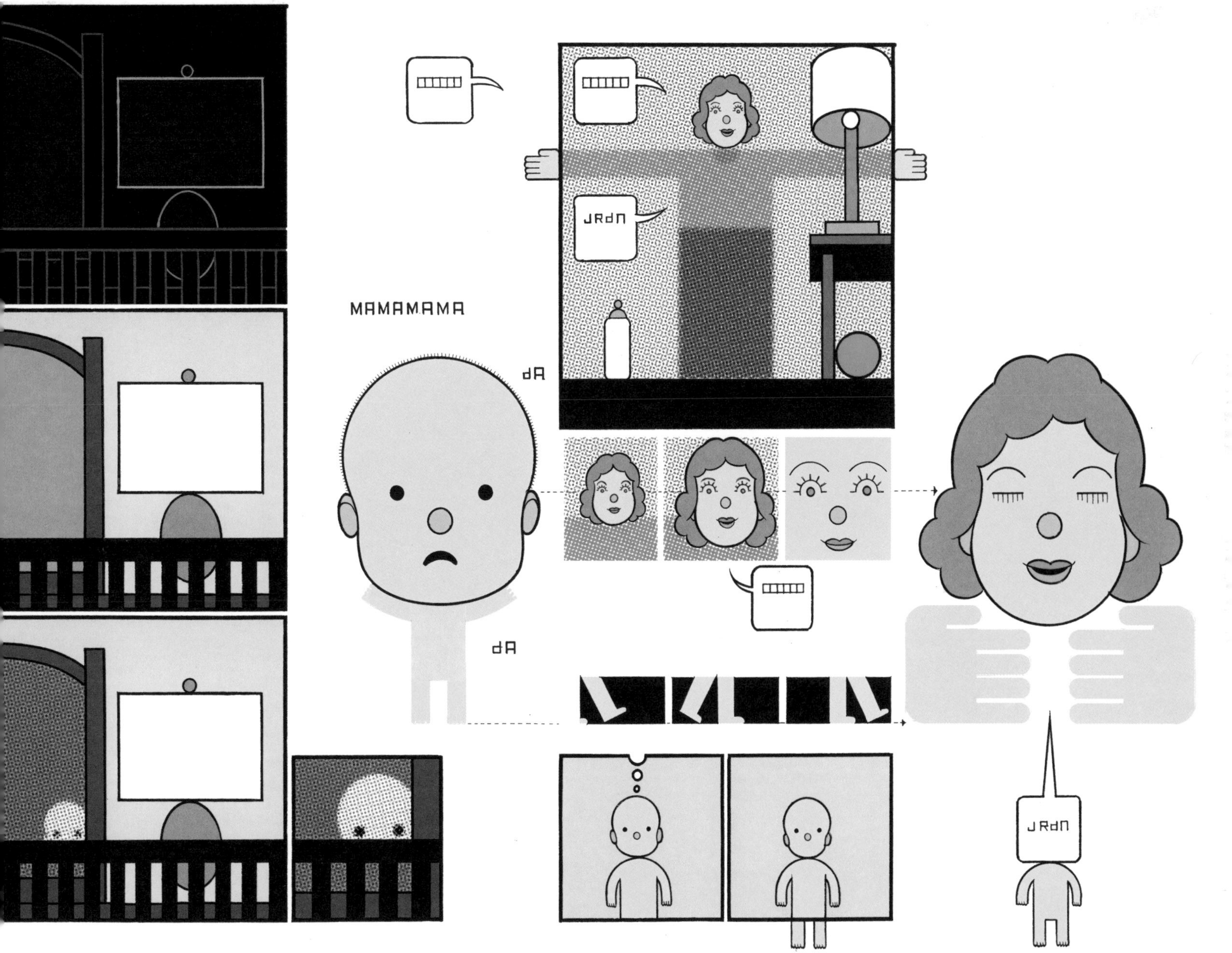

JRdn
MAMAMAMA
dA
dA
JRdn

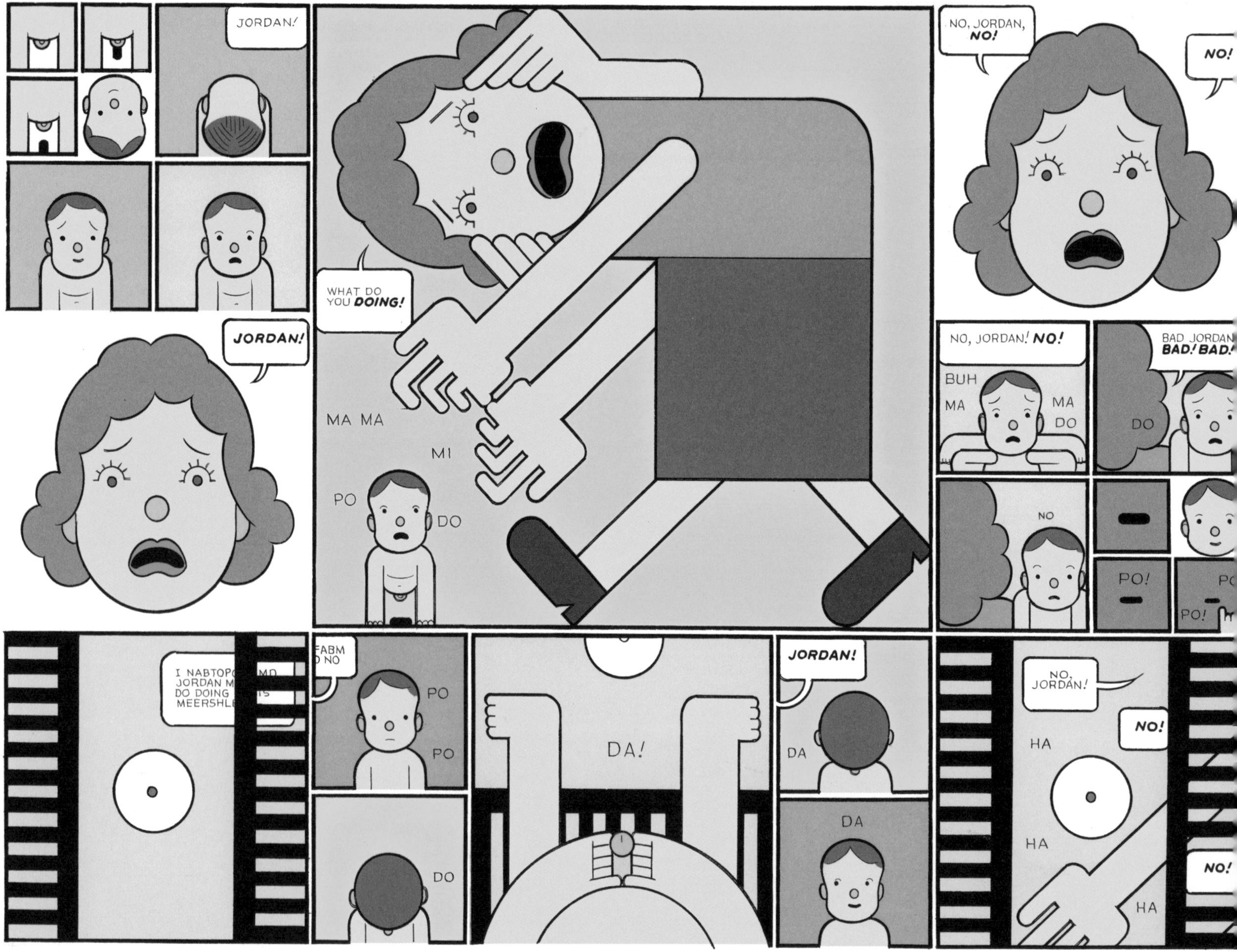
JORDAN!
JORDAN!
WHAT DO YOU DOING!
MA MA
MI
PO
DO
NO, JORDAN, NO!
NO!
NO, JORDAN! NO!
BUH
MA
MA
DO
BAD JORDAN BAD! BAD!
DO
NO
PO!
PO!
I NABTOPO MD JORDAN M DO DOING MEERSHLE
FABM NO
PO
PO
DO
DA!
JORDAN!
DA
DA
NO, JORDAN!
NO!
HA
HA
HA
NO!

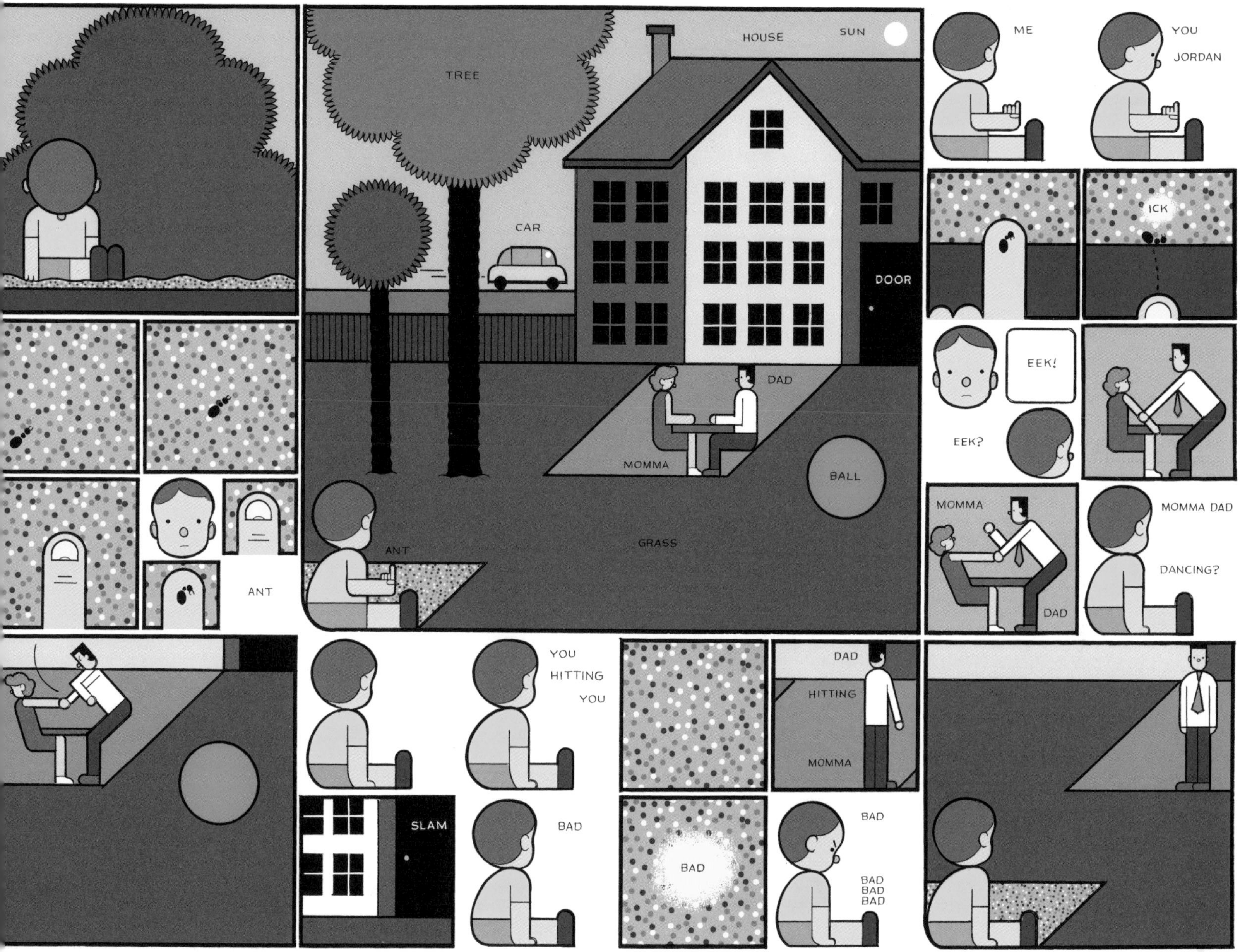

ANT
TREE
HOUSE
SUN
CAR
DOOR
DAD
MOMMA
BALL
ANT
GRASS
ME
YOU
JORDAN
ICK
EEK!
EEK?
MOMMA
DAD
MOMMA DAD
DANCING?
YOU
HITTING
YOU
SLAM
BAD
BAD
DAD
HITTING
MOMMA
BAD
BAD
BAD
BAD

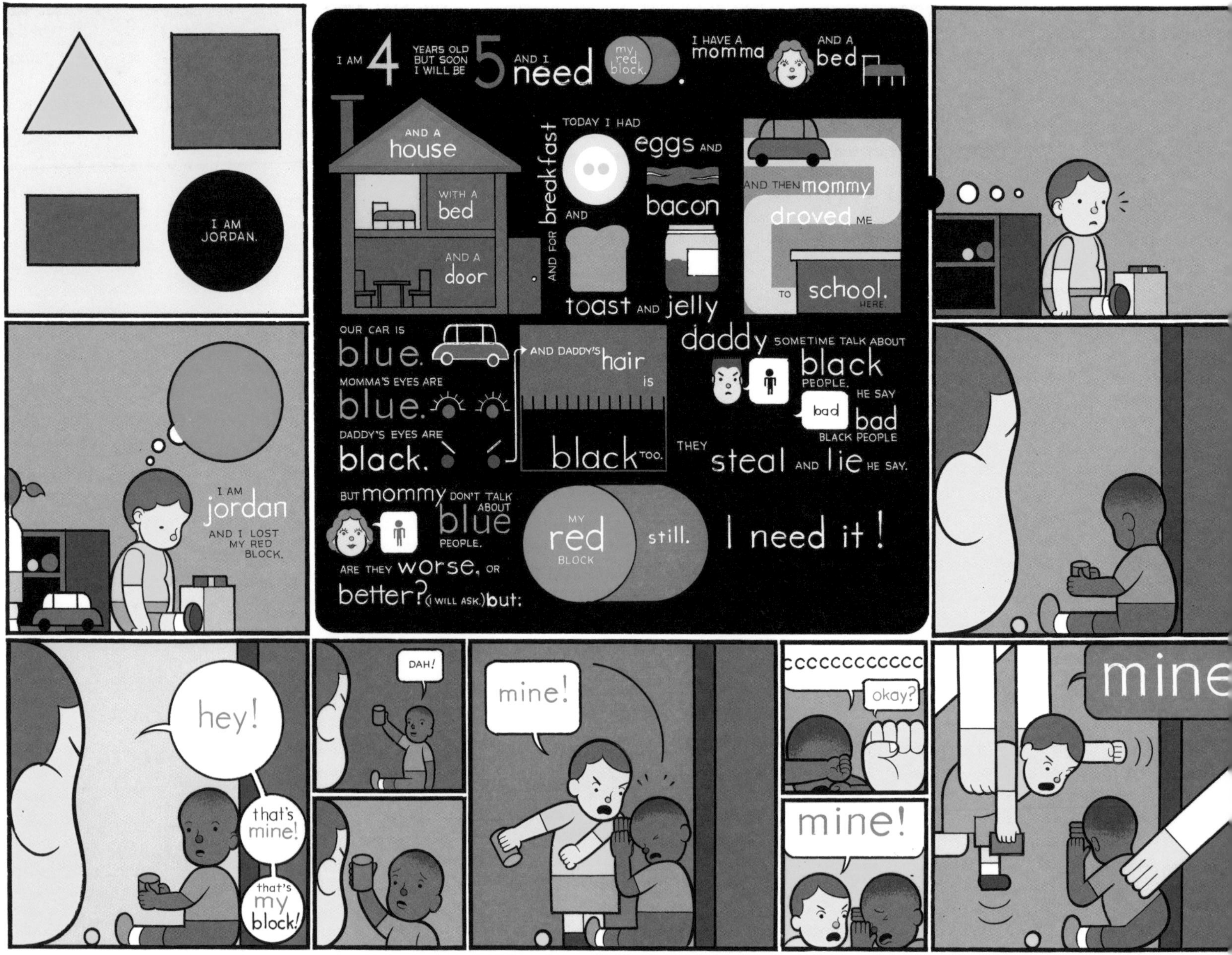

I AM JORDAN.
I AM jordan
AND I LOST MY RED BLOCK.
I AM 4 YEARS OLD BUT SOON I WILL BE 5 AND I need my red block.
I HAVE A momma AND A bed
AND A house
WITH A bed
AND A door
TODAY I HAD eggs AND bacon AND toast AND jelly AND FOR breakfast
AND THEN mommy droved ME TO school. HERE.
OUR CAR IS blue.
MOMMA'S EYES ARE blue.
DADDY'S EYES ARE black.
AND DADDY'S hair is black TOO.
daddy SOMETIME TALK ABOUT black PEOPLE. HE SAY bad
bad
BLACK PEOPLE
THEY steal AND lie HE SAY.
BUT mommy DON'T TALK ABOUT blue PEOPLE.
ARE THEY worse, OR better? (I WILL ASK.) but:
MY red BLOCK still.
I need it!
hey!
that's mine!
that's my block!
DAH!
mine!
cccccccccccc
okay?
mine!
mine

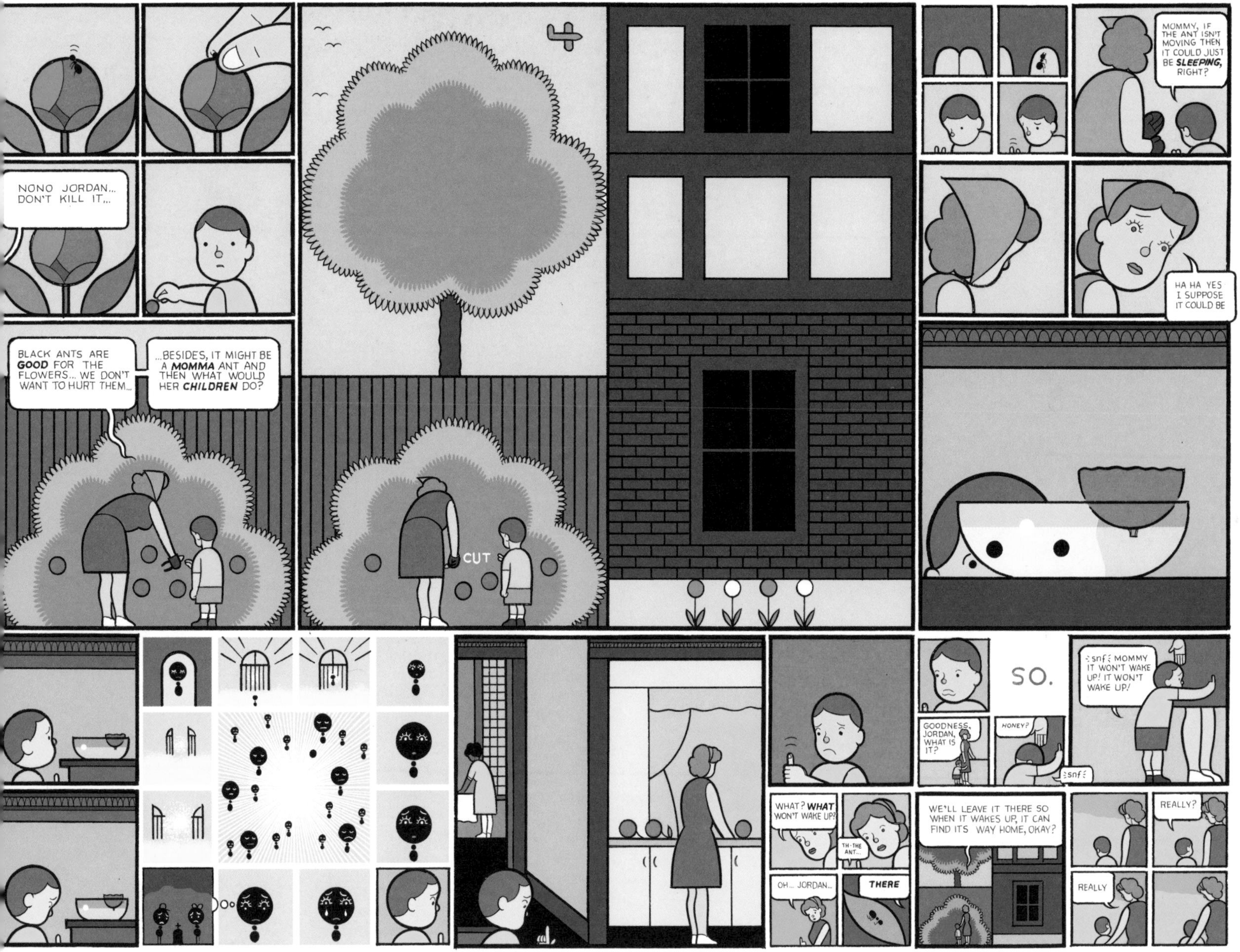
NONO JORDAN... DON'T KILL IT...
BLACK ANTS ARE **GOOD** FOR THE FLOWERS... WE DON'T WANT TO HURT THEM...
...BESIDES, IT MIGHT BE A **MOMMA** ANT AND THEN WHAT WOULD HER **CHILDREN** DO?
CUT
MOMMY, IF THE ANT ISN'T MOVING THEN IT COULD JUST BE ***SLEEPING,*** RIGHT?
HA HA YES I SUPPOSE IT COULD BE
SO.
GOODNESS, JORDAN, WHAT IS IT?
HONEY?
snf
snf MOMMY IT WON'T WAKE UP! IT WON'T WAKE UP!
WHAT? **WHAT** WON'T WAKE UP?
TH-THE ANT...
OH... JORDAN...
THERE
WE'LL LEAVE IT THERE SO WHEN IT WAKES UP, IT CAN FIND ITS WAY HOME, OKAY?
REALLY?
REALLY

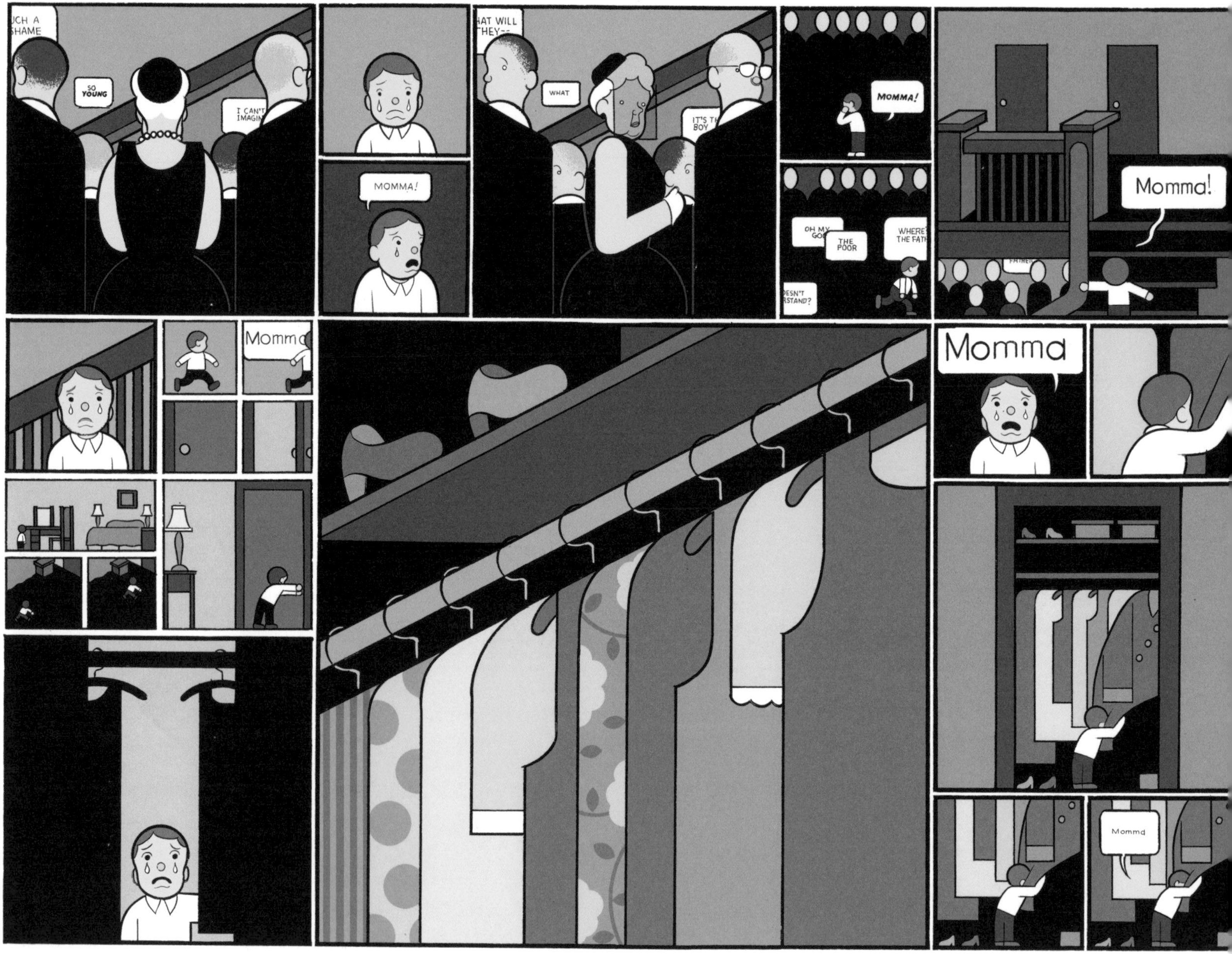

UCH A SHAME
SO YOUNG
I CAN'T IMAGIN
MOMMA!
HAT WILL THEY--
WHAT
IT'S TH BOY
MOMMA!
OH MY GO
THE POOR
WHERE? THE FATH
ESN'T RSTAND?
FATHER
Momma!
Momma
Momma
Momma

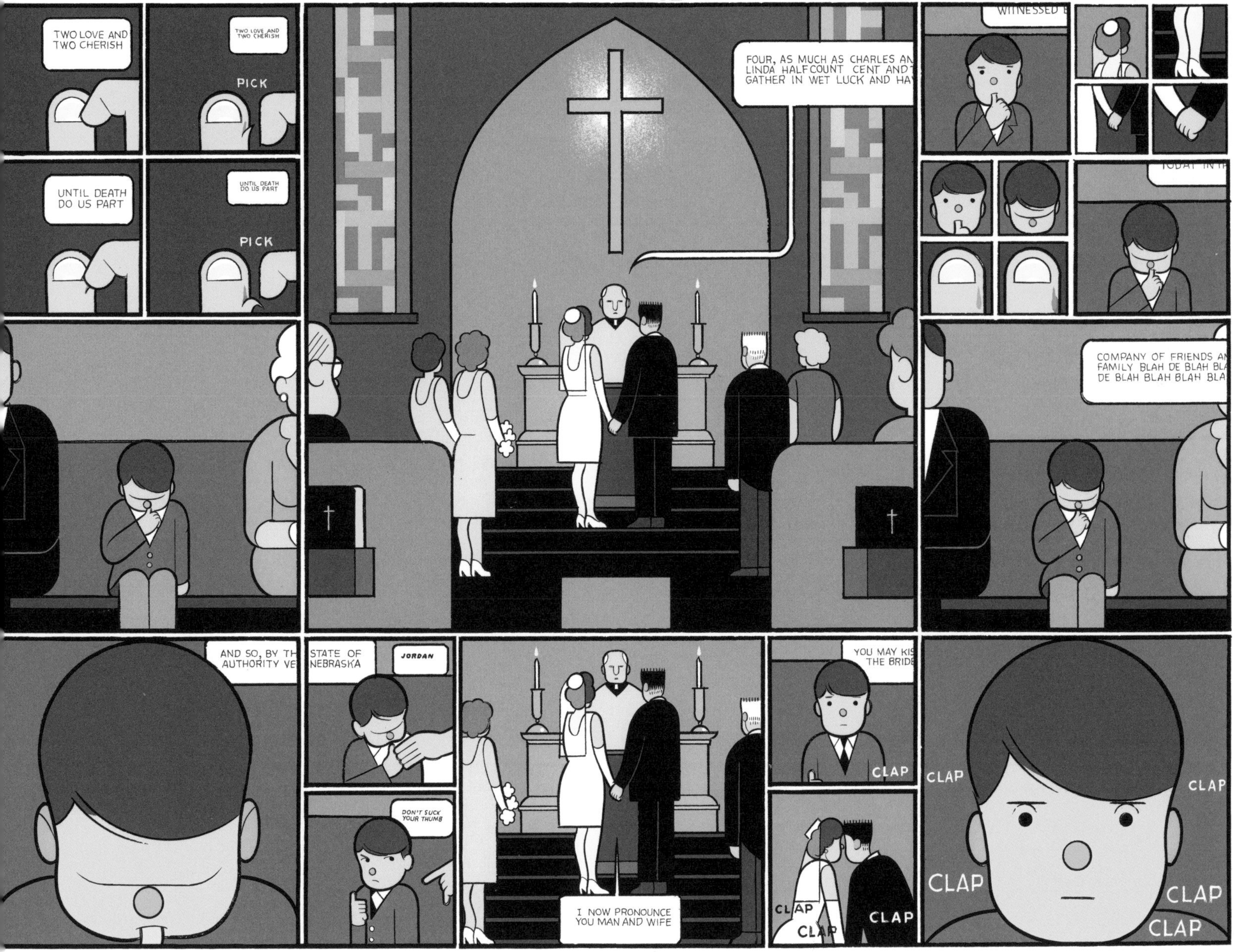
TWO LOVE AND TWO CHERISH
TWO LOVE AND TWO CHERISH
PICK
UNTIL DEATH DO US PART
UNTIL DEATH DO US PART
PICK
FOUR, AS MUCH AS CHARLES AN LINDA HALFCOUNT CENT AND T GATHER IN WET LUCK AND HA
WITNESSED B
TODAY IN TH
COMPANY OF FRIENDS AN FAMILY BLAH DE BLAH BLA DE BLAH BLAH BLAH BLA
AND SO, BY TH AUTHORITY VE
STATE OF NEBRASKA
JORDAN
DON'T SUCK YOUR THUMB
I NOW PRONOUNCE YOU MAN AND WIFE
YOU MAY KIS THE BRIDE
CLAP
CLAP
CLAP
CLAP
CLAP
CLAP
CLAP
CLAP
CLAP

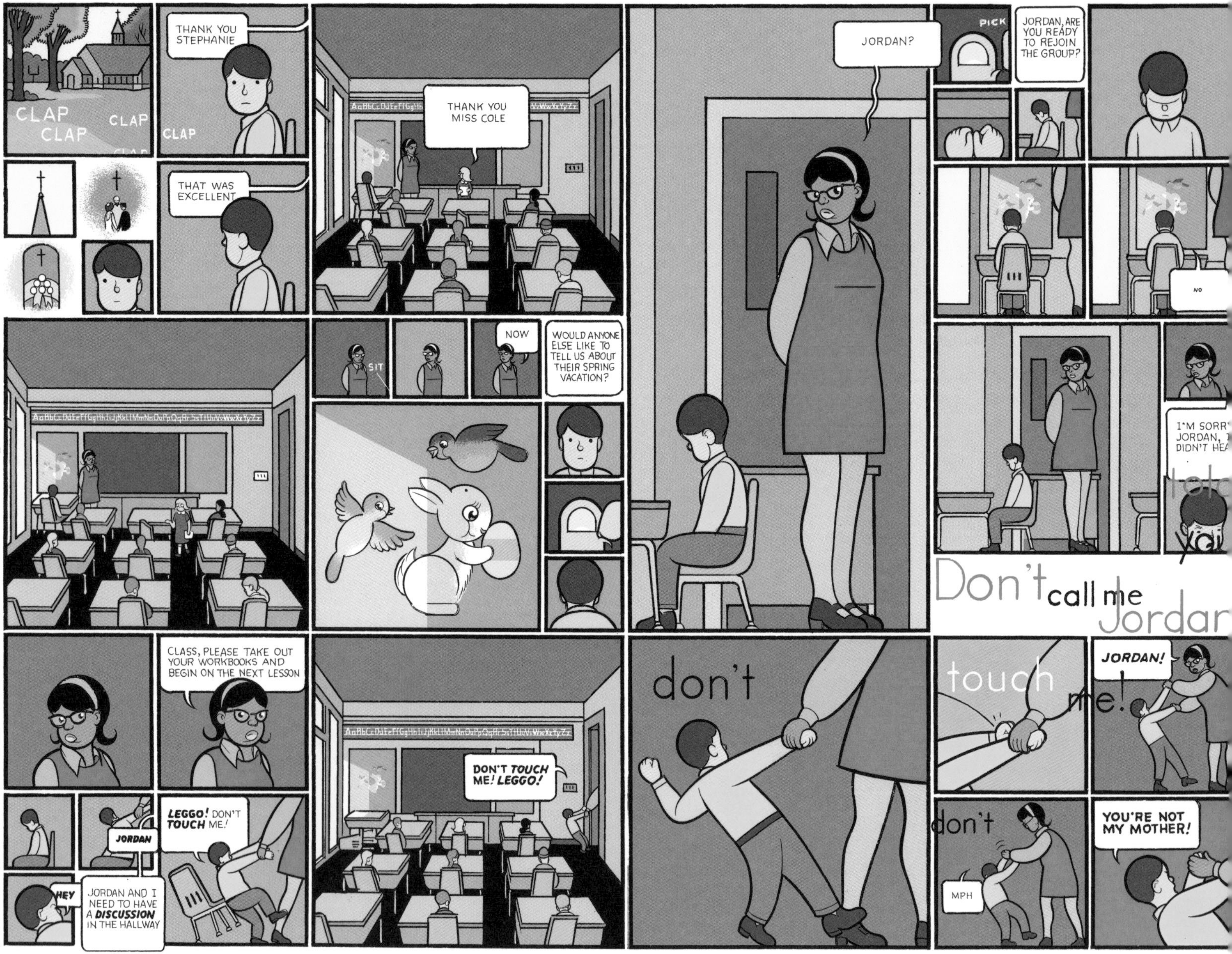
CLAP
CLAP
CLAP
CLAP
THANK YOU STEPHANIE
THAT WAS EXCELLENT
THANK YOU MISS COLE
SIT
NOW
WOULD ANYONE ELSE LIKE TO TELL US ABOUT THEIR SPRING VACATION?
JORDAN?
PICK
JORDAN, ARE YOU READY TO REJOIN THE GROUP?
NO
I'M SORR
JORDAN, I
DIDN'T HEA
Don't call me Jordan
CLASS, PLEASE TAKE OUT YOUR WORKBOOKS AND BEGIN ON THE NEXT LESSON
JORDAN
HEY
JORDAN AND I NEED TO HAVE A DISCUSSION IN THE HALLWAY
LEGGO! DON'T TOUCH ME!
DON'T TOUCH ME! LEGGO!
don't
touch me!
JORDAN!
don't
MPH
YOU'RE NOT MY MOTHER!

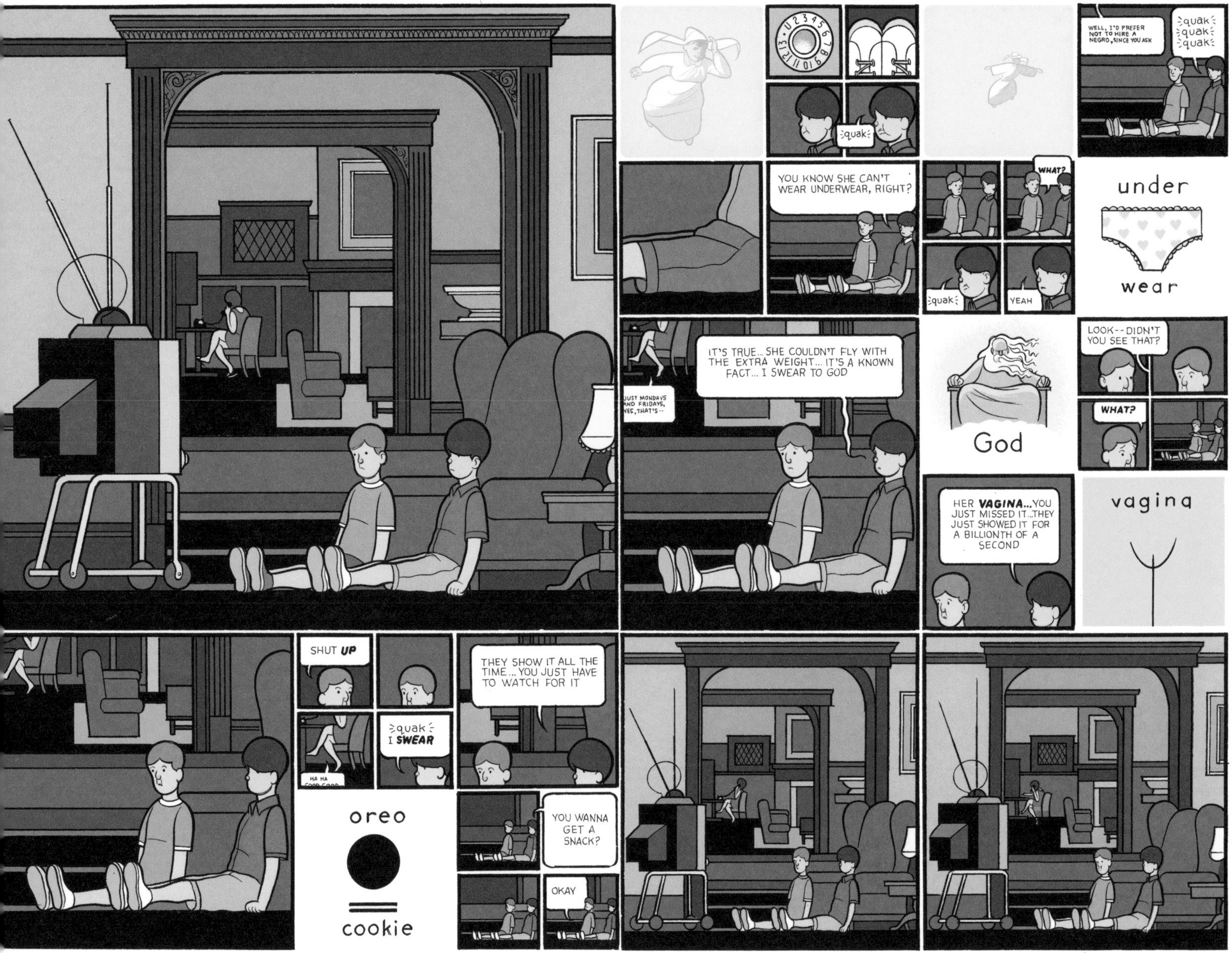
quak
WELL, I'D PREFER NOT TO HIRE A NEGRO, SINCE YOU ASK
quak quak quak
YOU KNOW SHE CAN'T WEAR UNDERWEAR, RIGHT?
WHAT?
quak
YEAH
under
wear
JUST MONDAYS AND FRIDAYS, YES, THAT'S--
IT'S TRUE... SHE COULDN'T FLY WITH THE EXTRA WEIGHT... IT'S A KNOWN FACT... I SWEAR TO GOD
God
LOOK--DIDN'T YOU SEE THAT?
WHAT?
HER VAGINA... YOU JUST MISSED IT... THEY JUST SHOWED IT FOR A BILLIONTH OF A SECOND
vagina
SHUT UP
HA HA
quak I SWEAR
oreo
cookie
THEY SHOW IT ALL THE TIME... YOU JUST HAVE TO WATCH FOR IT
YOU WANNA GET A SNACK?
OKAY

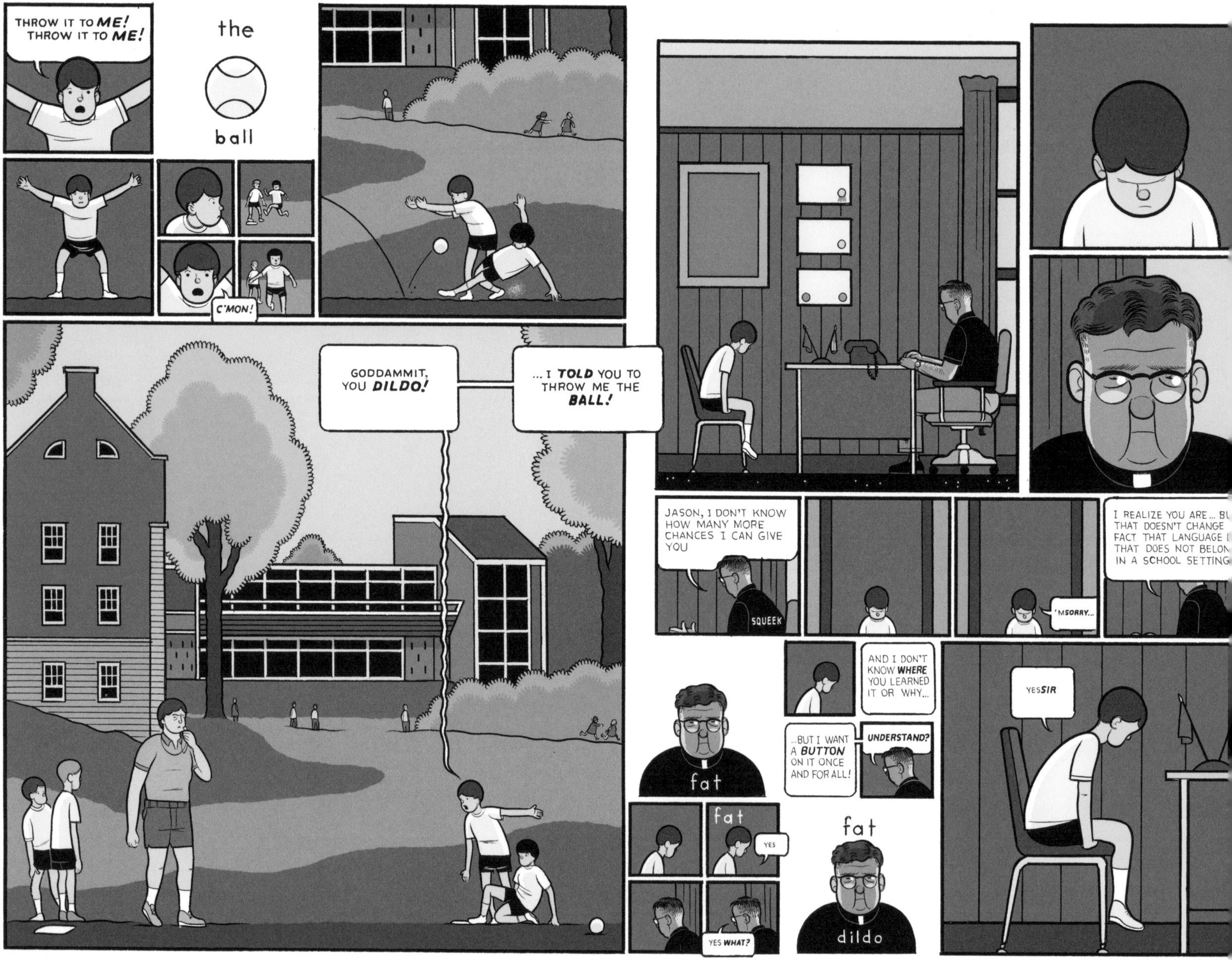
THROW IT TO ME! THROW IT TO ME!
the ball
C'MON!
GODDAMMIT, YOU DILDO!
... I TOLD YOU TO THROW ME THE BALL!
JASON, I DON'T KNOW HOW MANY MORE CHANCES I CAN GIVE YOU
SQUEEK
'MSORRY...
I REALIZE YOU ARE... BU
THAT DOESN'T CHANGE
FACT THAT LANGUAGE I
THAT DOES NOT BELON
IN A SCHOOL SETTING
AND I DON'T KNOW WHERE YOU LEARNED IT OR WHY...
...BUT I WANT A BUTTON ON IT ONCE AND FOR ALL!
UNDERSTAND?
fat
fat
YES
YES WHAT?
fat
dildo
YESSIR

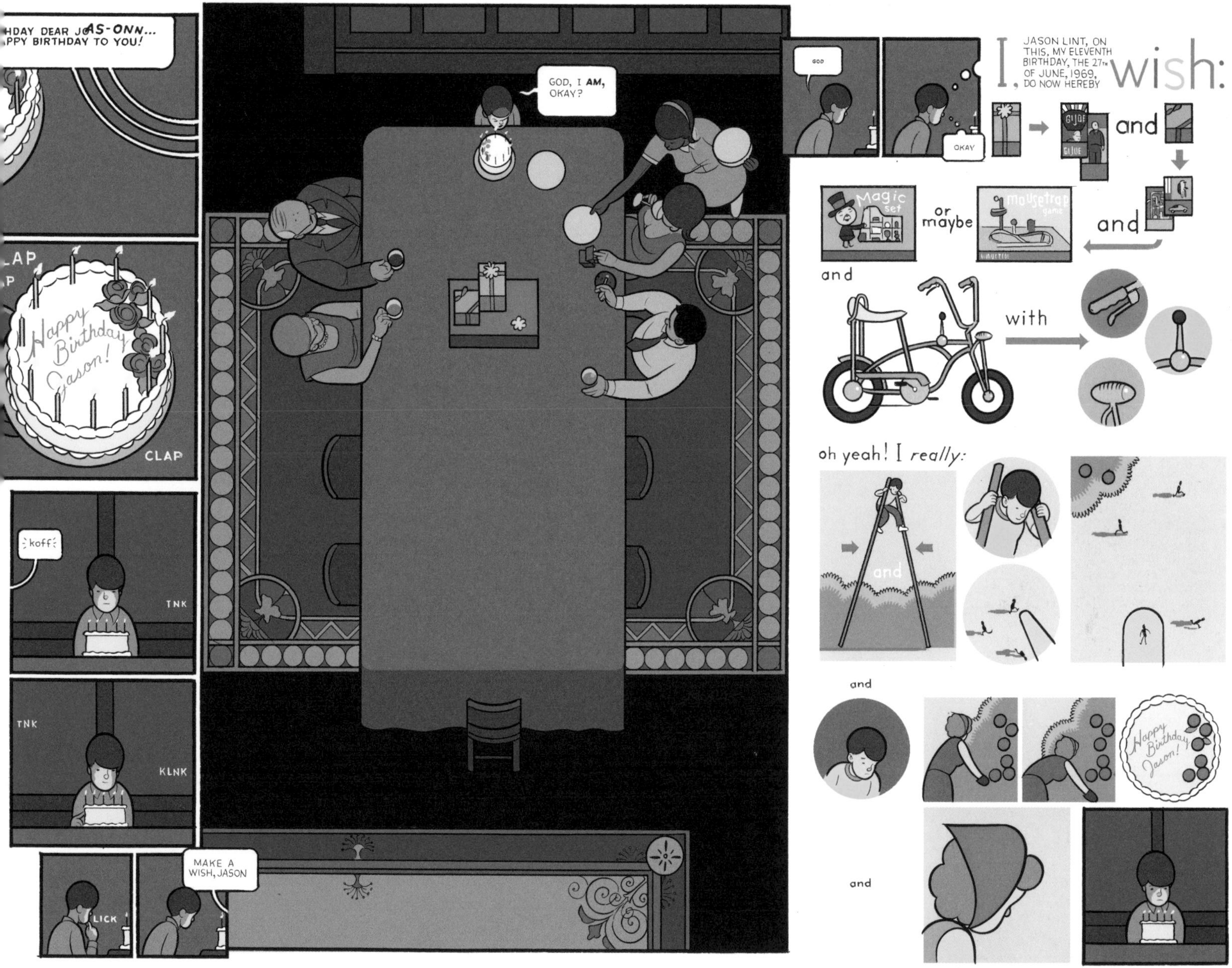

HDAY DEAR JAS-ONN...
PPY BIRTHDAY TO YOU!
LAP
P
Happy Birthday Jason!
CLAP
koff
TNK
TNK
KLNK
LICK
MAKE A WISH, JASON
GOD, I AM, OKAY?
GOD
OKAY
I, JASON LINT, ON THIS, MY ELEVENTH BIRTHDAY, THE 27TH OF JUNE, 1969, DO NOW HEREBY wish:
and
Magic set
or maybe
mousetrap game
and
and
with
oh yeah! I really:
and
and
Happy Birthday Jason!
and

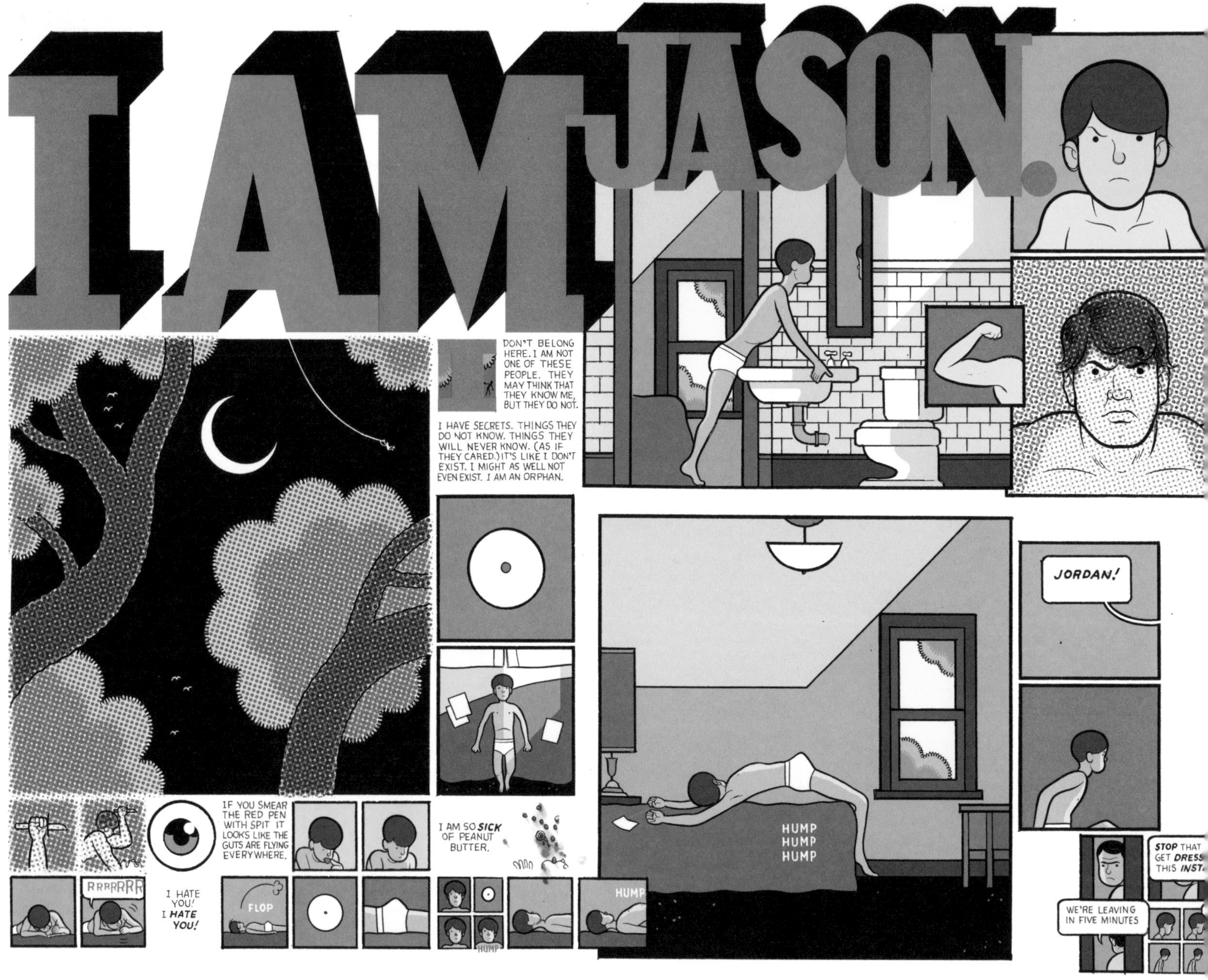
I AM JASON.
DON'T BELONG HERE. I AM NOT ONE OF THESE PEOPLE. THEY MAY THINK THAT THEY KNOW ME, BUT THEY DO NOT.
I HAVE SECRETS. THINGS THEY DO NOT KNOW. THINGS THEY WILL NEVER KNOW. (AS IF THEY CARED.) IT'S LIKE I DON'T EXIST. I MIGHT AS WELL NOT EVEN EXIST. I AM AN ORPHAN.
JORDAN!
IF YOU SMEAR THE RED PEN WITH SPIT IT LOOKS LIKE THE GUTS ARE FLYING EVERYWHERE.
I AM SO SICK OF PEANUT BUTTER.
HUMP HUMP HUMP
RRRRRRR
I HATE YOU! I HATE YOU!
FLOP
HUMP
HUMP
WE'RE LEAVING IN FIVE MINUTES

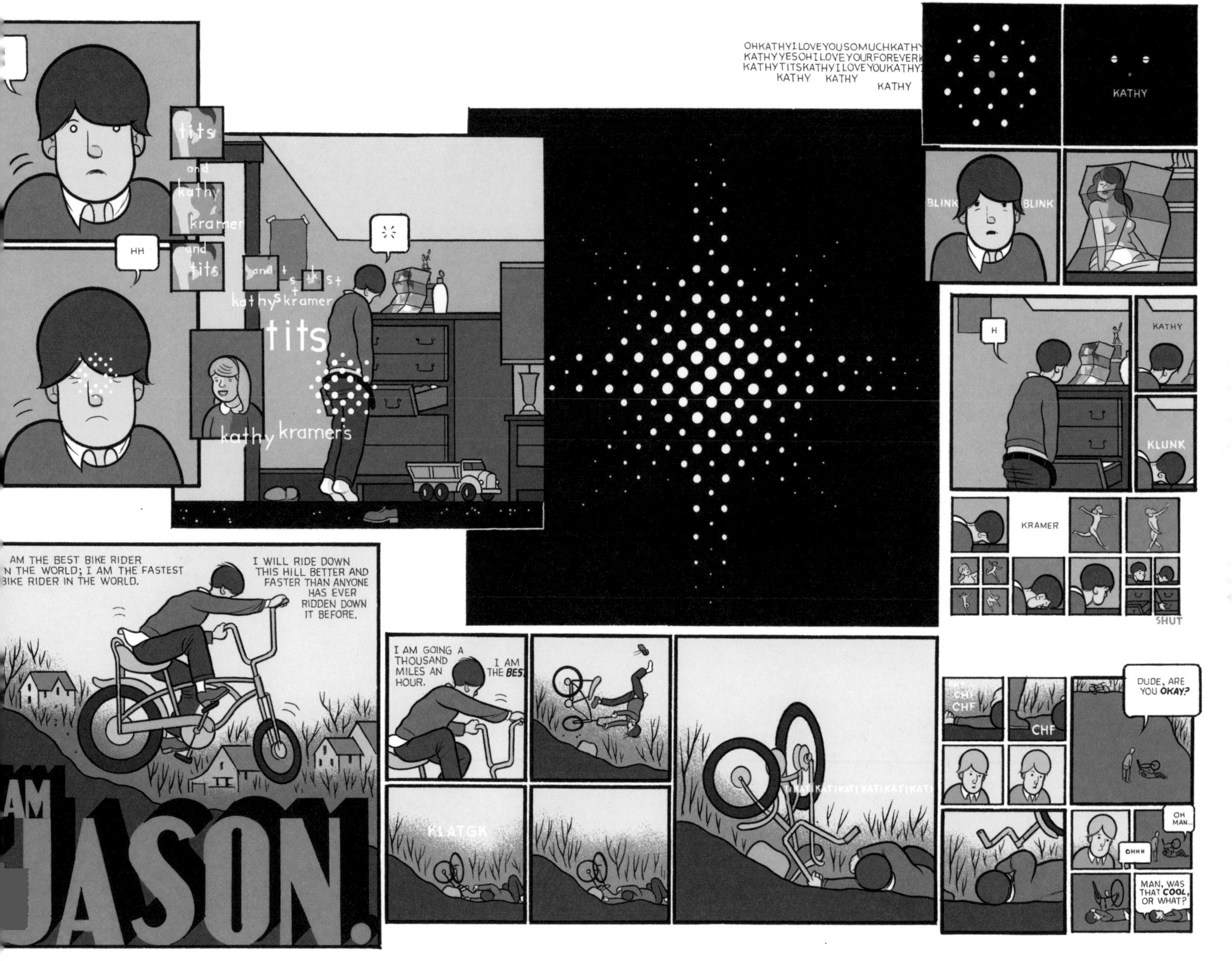

HH
tits
and
kathy
kramer
and
tits
and
kathy kramer
tits
kathy kramers
OHKATHYILOVEYOUSOMUCHKATHY
KATHYYESOHILOVEYOURFOREVERK
KATHYTITSKATHYILOVEYOUKATHYI
KATHY KATHY KATHY
KATHY
BLINK
BLINK
H
KATHY
KLUNK
KRAMER
SHUT
AM THE BEST BIKE RIDER
N THE WORLD; I AM THE FASTEST
BIKE RIDER IN THE WORLD.
I WILL RIDE DOWN THIS HILL BETTER AND FASTER THAN ANYONE HAS EVER RIDDEN DOWN IT BEFORE.
AM JASON.
I AM GOING A THOUSAND MILES AN HOUR.
I AM THE BEST
KLATGK
CHF
CHF
DUDE, ARE YOU OKAY?
OH MAN...
OHHH
MAN, WAS THAT COOL, OR WHAT?

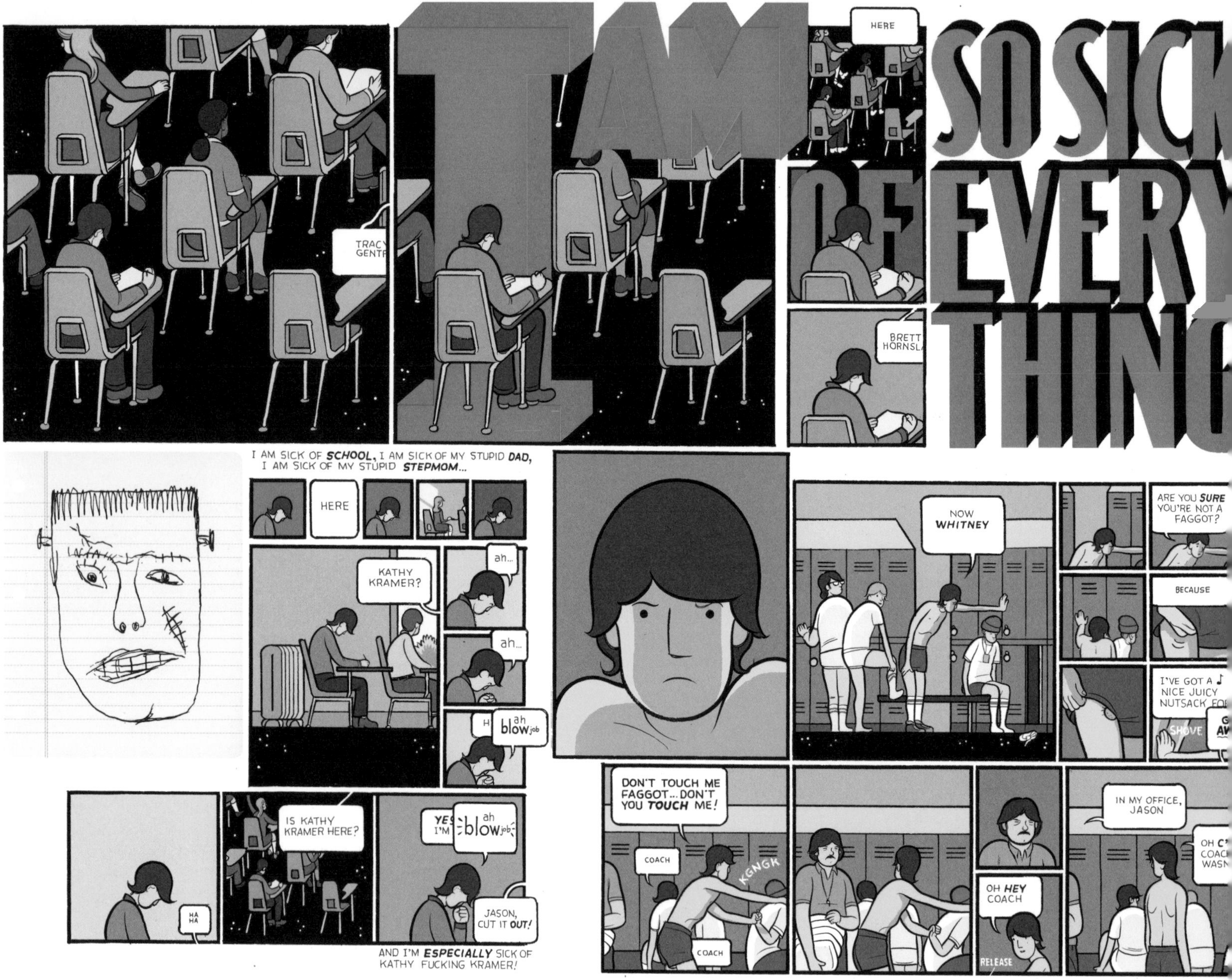
TRACY GENTR
I AM
SO SICK OF EVERY THING
HERE
BRETT HORNSLA
I AM SICK OF SCHOOL, I AM SICK OF MY STUPID DAD, I AM SICK OF MY STUPID STEPMOM...
HERE
KATHY KRAMER?
ah...
ah...
ah blowjob
HA HA
IS KATHY KRAMER HERE?
YES I'M
ah blowjob
JASON, CUT IT OUT!
AND I'M ESPECIALLY SICK OF KATHY FUCKING KRAMER!
NOW WHITNEY
ARE YOU SURE YOU'RE NOT A FAGGOT?
BECAUSE
I'VE GOT A NICE JUICY NUTSACK FO
SHOVE
DON'T TOUCH ME FAGGOT... DON'T YOU TOUCH ME!
COACH
KGNGK
COACH
OH HEY COACH
RELEASE
IN MY OFFICE, JASON
OH C' COACH WASN

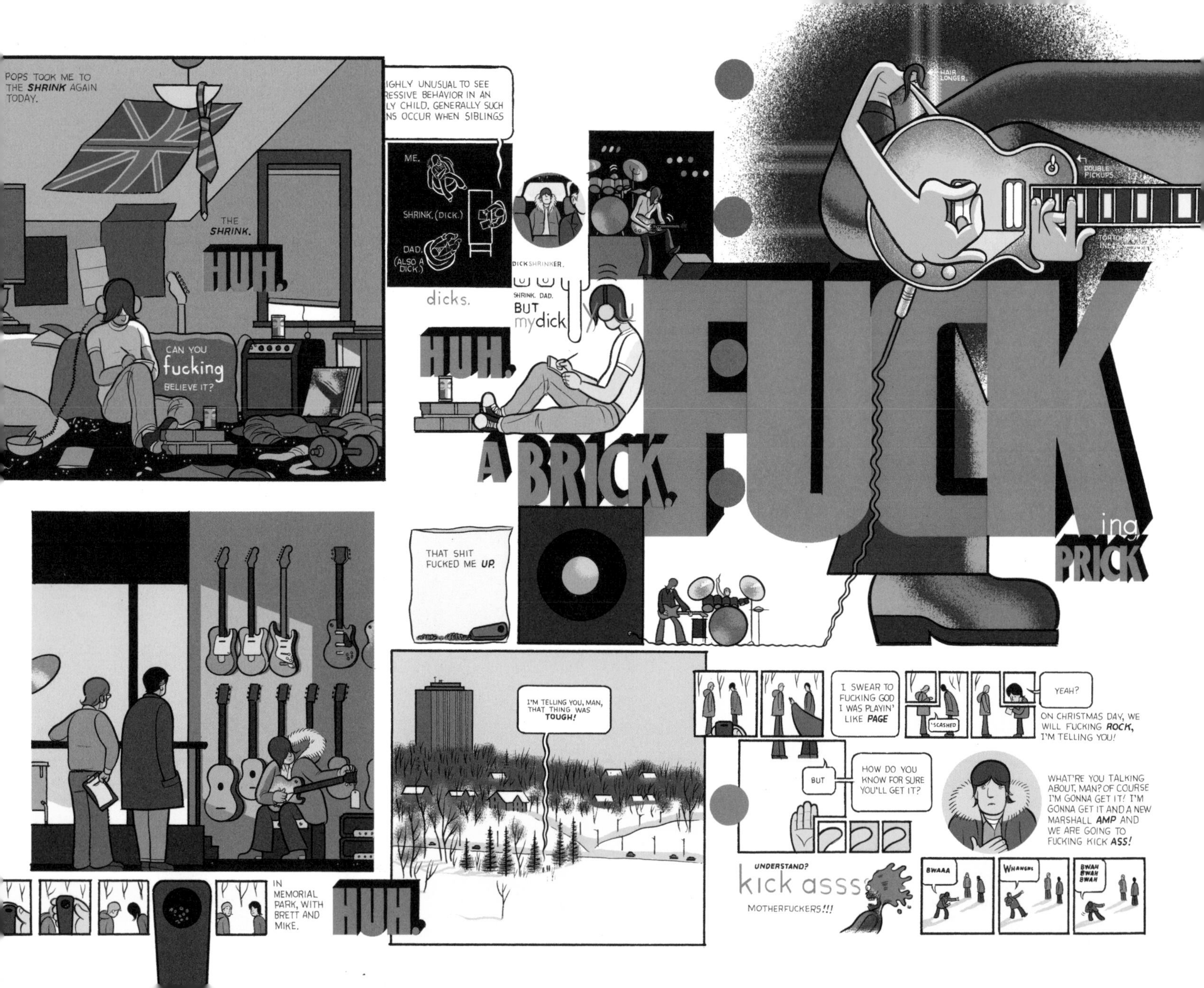
POPS TOOK ME TO THE SHRINK AGAIN TODAY.
THE SHRINK.
HUH.
CAN YOU fucking BELIEVE IT?
IGHLY UNUSUAL TO SEE
RESSIVE BEHAVIOR IN AN
LY CHILD. GENERALLY SUCH
NS OCCUR WHEN SIBLINGS
ME.
SHRINK. (DICK.)
DAD. (ALSO A DICK.)
DICKSHRINKER.
dicks.
SHRINK. DAD.
BUT
mydick
You
HUH.
A BRICK.
FUCK
ing
PRICK
HAIR LONGER.
DOUBLE PICKUPS.
THAT SHIT FUCKED ME UP.
I'M TELLING YOU, MAN, THAT THING WAS TOUGH!
I SWEAR TO FUCKING GOD I WAS PLAYIN' LIKE PAGE
'SCASHED
YEAH?
ON CHRISTMAS DAY, WE WILL FUCKING ROCK, I'M TELLING YOU!
BUT
HOW DO YOU KNOW FOR SURE YOU'LL GET IT?
WHAT'RE YOU TALKING ABOUT, MAN? OF COURSE I'M GONNA GET IT! I'M GONNA GET IT AND A NEW MARSHALL AMP AND WE ARE GOING TO FUCKING KICK ASS!
UNDERSTAND?
kick asss
MOTHERFUCKERS!!!
BWAAA
WHANG
BWAH BWAH BWAH
IN MEMORIAL PARK, WITH BRETT AND MIKE.
HUH.

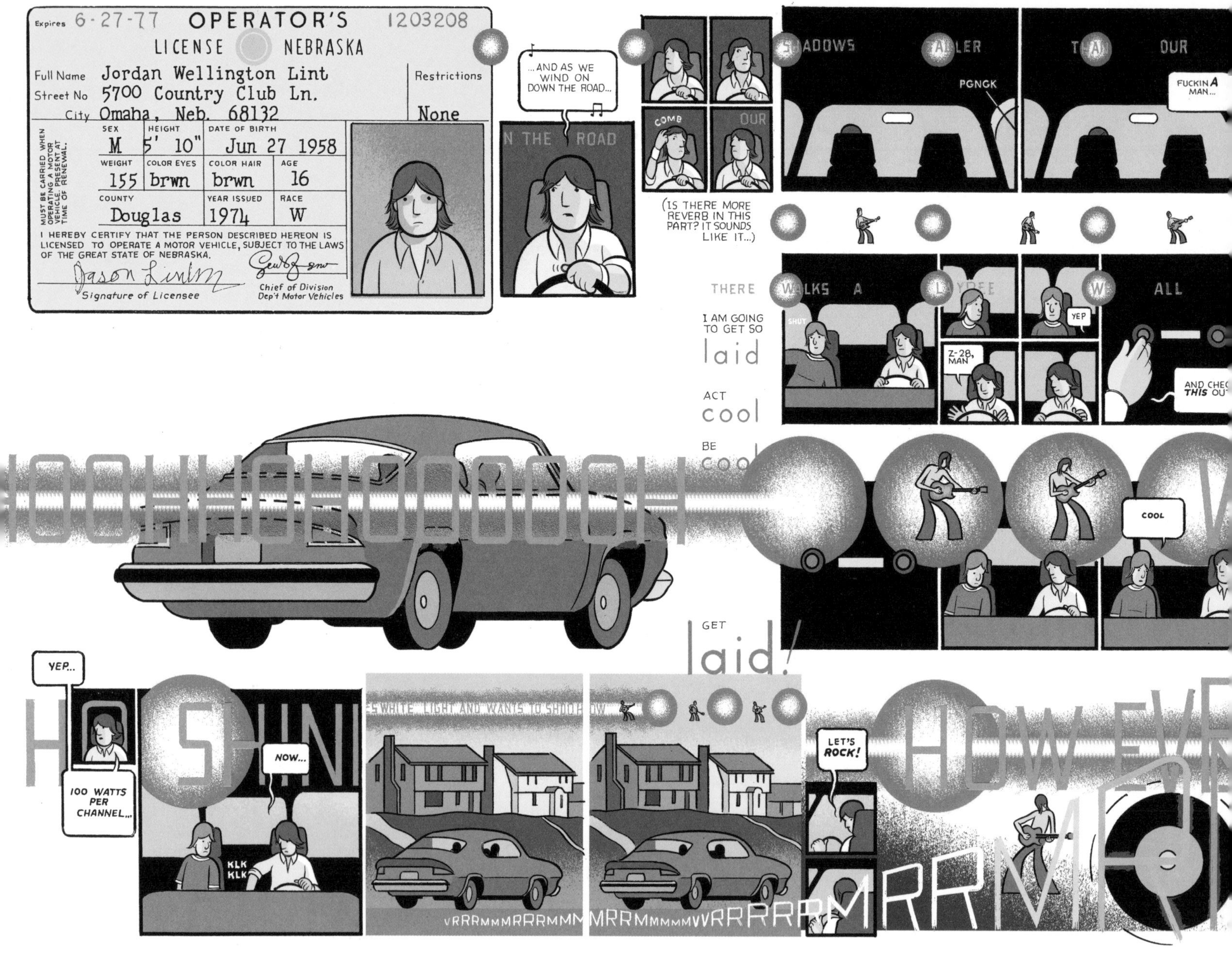

Expires 6-27-77 OPERATOR'S 1203208
LICENSE NEBRASKA
Full Name Jordan Wellington Lint
Street No 5700 Country Club Ln.
City Omaha, Neb. 68132
Restrictions
None
SEX M
HEIGHT 5' 10"
DATE OF BIRTH Jun 27 1958
WEIGHT 155
COLOR EYES brwn
COLOR HAIR brwn
AGE 16
COUNTY Douglas
YEAR ISSUED 1974
RACE W
MUST BE CARRIED WHEN OPERATING A MOTOR VEHICLE. PRESENT AT TIME OF RENEWAL.
I HEREBY CERTIFY THAT THE PERSON DESCRIBED HEREON IS LICENSED TO OPERATE A MOTOR VEHICLE, SUBJECT TO THE LAWS OF THE GREAT STATE OF NEBRASKA.
Jason Lint
Signature of Licensee
Chief of Division
Dep't Motor Vehicles
...AND AS WE WIND ON DOWN THE ROAD...
N THE ROAD
COMB
OUR
(IS THERE MORE REVERB IN THIS PART? IT SOUNDS LIKE IT...)
ADOWS
LER
OUR
PGNGK
FUCKIN A MAN...
THERE
LKS
A
ALL
I AM GOING TO GET SO
laid
ACT
cool
BE
coo
SHUT
YEP
Z-28, MAN
AND CHEC THIS OU
COOL
GET
laid!
YEP...
100 WATTS PER CHANNEL...
NOW...
KLK KLK
WHITE LIGHT AND WANTS TO SHOW HOW
VRRRMMMRRRMMMMRRMMMMMVVRRRRRM
LET'S ROCK!
MRRRM

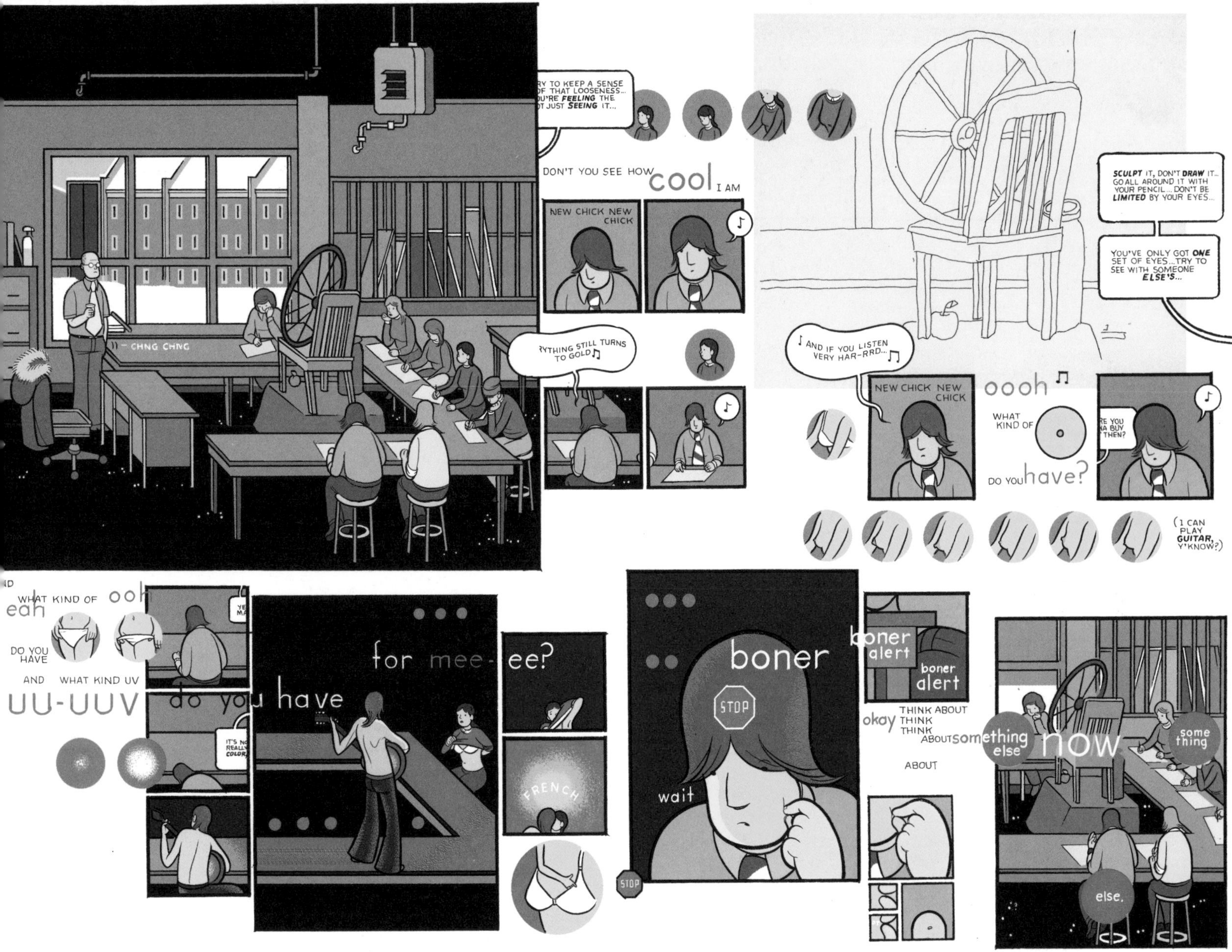

— CHNG CHNG
RY TO KEEP A SENSE OF THAT LOOSENESS... OU'RE FEELING THE OT JUST SEEING IT...
DON'T YOU SEE HOW cool I AM
NEW CHICK NEW CHICK
RYTHING STILL TURNS TO GOLD
SCULPT IT, DON'T DRAW IT... GO ALL AROUND IT WITH YOUR PENCIL... DON'T BE LIMITED BY YOUR EYES...
YOU'VE ONLY GOT ONE SET OF EYES... TRY TO SEE WITH SOMEONE ELSE'S...
AND IF YOU LISTEN VERY HAR-RRD...
NEW CHICK NEW CHICK
oooh
WHAT KIND OF
DO YOU have?
RE YOU NA BUY THEN?
(I CAN PLAY GUITAR, Y'KNOW?)
WHAT KIND OF ooh eah
DO YOU HAVE
AND WHAT KIND UV
UU-UUV
do you have
for mee-ee?
FRENCH
boner
STOP
wait
STOP
boner alert
boner alert
okay THINK ABOUT THINK THINK ABOUT something else
ABOUT
now
some thing
else.

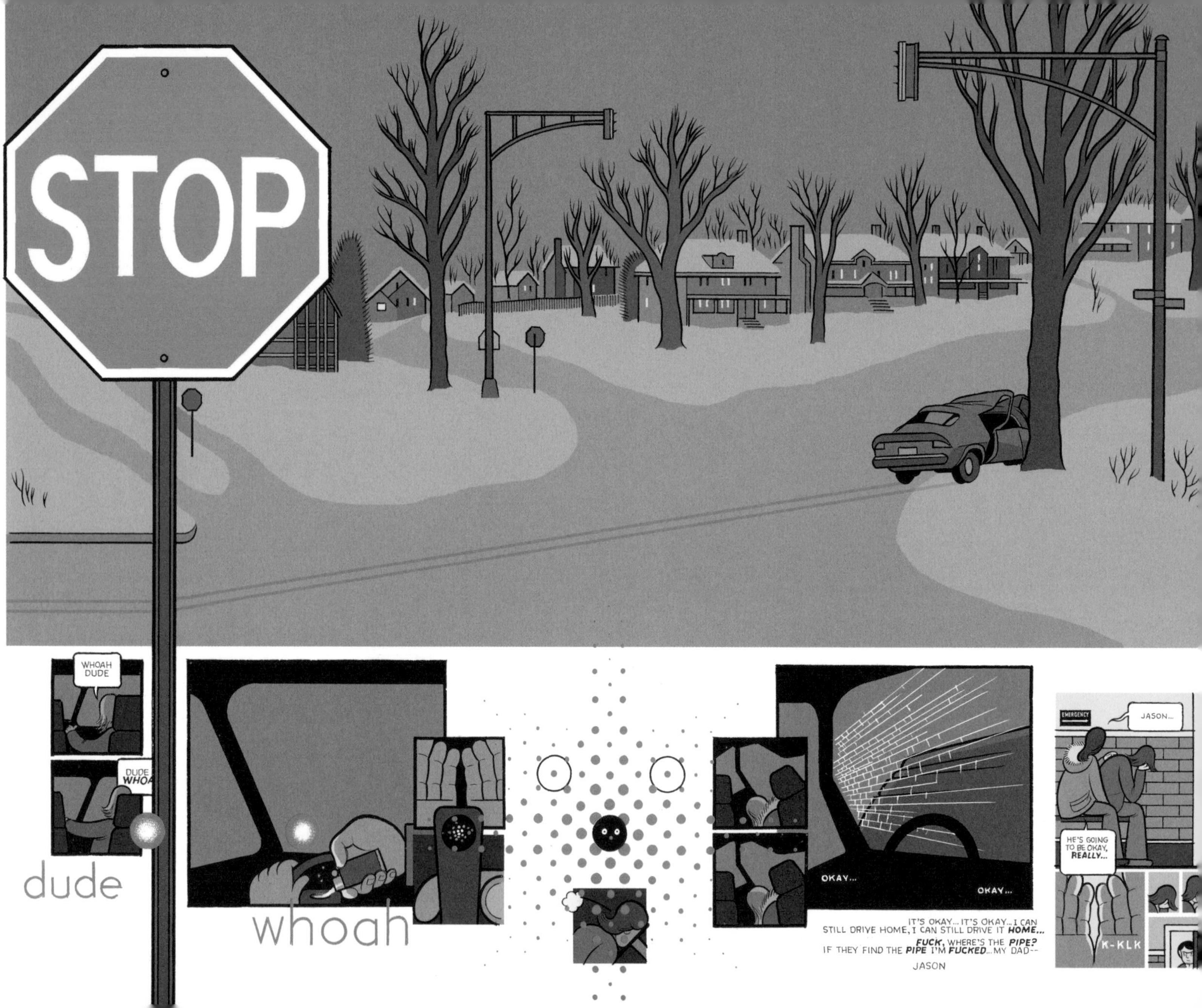
STOP
WHOAH DUDE
DUDE WHOA
dude
whoah
OKAY...
OKAY...
IT'S OKAY... IT'S OKAY... I CAN STILL DRIVE HOME, I CAN STILL DRIVE IT **HOME...**
FUCK, WHERE'S THE **PIPE?** IF THEY FIND THE **PIPE** I'M **FUCKED**... MY DAD--
JASON
EMERGENCY
JASON...
HE'S GOING TO BE OKAY, **REALLY...**
K-KLK

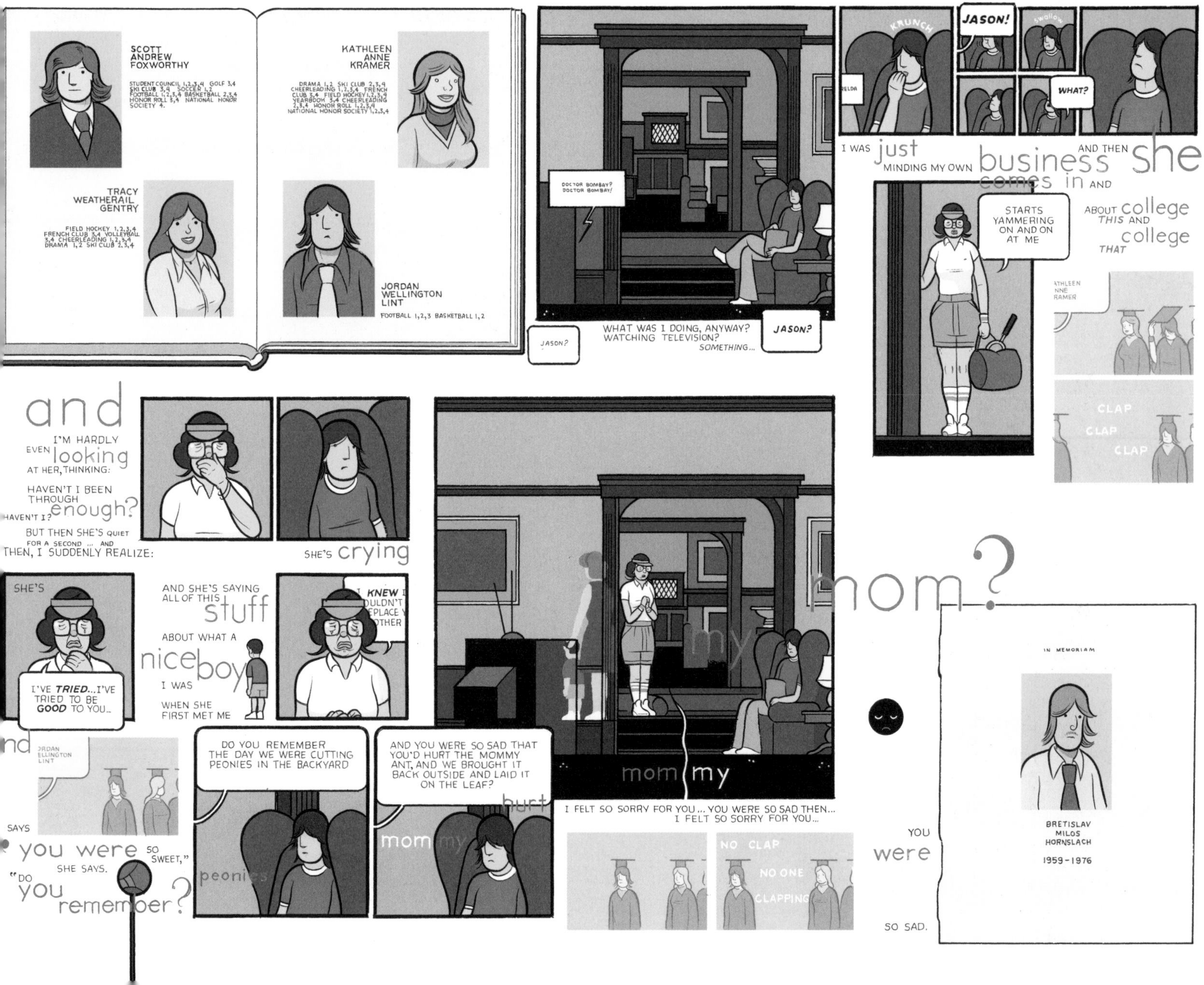
SCOTT ANDREW FOXWORTHY
STUDENT COUNCIL 1,2,3,4 GOLF 3,4 SKI CLUB 3,4 SOCCER 1,2 FOOTBALL 1,2,3,4 BASKETBALL 2,3,4 HONOR ROLL 3,4 NATIONAL HONOR SOCIETY 4.
KATHLEEN ANNE KRAMER
DRAMA 1,2 SKI CLUB 2,3,4 CHEERLEADING 1,2,3,4 FRENCH CLUB 3,4 FIELD HOCKEY 1,2,3,4 YEARBOOK 3,4 CHEERLEADING 2,3,4 HONOR ROLL 1,2,3,4 NATIONAL HONOR SOCIETY 1,2,3,4
TRACY WEATHERAIL GENTRY
FIELD HOCKEY 1,2,3,4 FRENCH CLUB 3,4 VOLLEYBALL 3,4 CHEERLEADING 1,2,3,4 DRAMA 1,2 SKI CLUB 2,3,4
JORDAN WELLINGTON LINT
FOOTBALL 1,2,3 BASKETBALL 1,2
DOCTOR BOMBAY? DOCTOR BOMBAY!
JASON?
WHAT WAS I DOING, ANYWAY? WATCHING TELEVISION? SOMETHING...
JASON?
KRUNCH
JASON!
swallow
WHAT?
I WAS just MINDING MY OWN business AND THEN she comes in AND
STARTS YAMMERING ON AND ON AT ME
ABOUT college THIS AND college THAT
CLAP CLAP CLAP
and I'M HARDLY EVEN looking AT HER, THINKING:
HAVEN'T I BEEN THROUGH enough? HAVEN'T I?
BUT THEN SHE'S QUIET FOR A SECOND ... AND THEN, I SUDDENLY REALIZE:
SHE'S crying
SHE'S
I'VE TRIED...I'VE TRIED TO BE GOOD TO YOU...
AND SHE'S SAYING ALL OF THIS stuff ABOUT WHAT A nice boy I WAS WHEN SHE FIRST MET ME
I KNEW I ...ULDN'T ...EPLACE Y... ...OTHER
my mom?
mom my
SAYS "you were SO SWEET," SHE SAYS. "DO you remember?
DO YOU REMEMBER THE DAY WE WERE CUTTING PEONIES IN THE BACKYARD
peonies
AND YOU WERE SO SAD THAT YOU'D HURT THE MOMMY ANT, AND WE BROUGHT IT BACK OUTSIDE AND LAID IT ON THE LEAF?
hurt
mom my
I FELT SO SORRY FOR YOU ... YOU WERE SO SAD THEN... I FELT SO SORRY FOR YOU...
NO CLAP NO ONE CLAPPING
YOU were SO SAD.
IN MEMORIAM
BRETISLAV MILOS HORNSLACH
1959-1976

my dad

NAH, DON'T WORRY ABOUT THIS... IT'S AN EASY ONE... WE'VE ALL DONE IT, RIGHT?

WARNED ME THAT I WOULDN'T AUTOMATICALLY BECOME A LAMBDA-DELT JUST BECAUSE I WAS LEGACY...

...AND YOU KNOW WHAT?

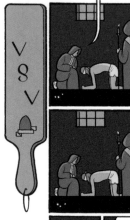

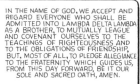

brothers,

IN THE NAME OF GOD, WE ACCEPT AND REGARD EVERYONE WHO SHALL BE ADMITTED INTO LAMBDA DELTA LAMBDA AS A BROTHER, TO MUTUALLY LEAGUE AND COVENANT OURSELVES TO THE TEACHINGS OF RIGHTEOUSNESS AND TO THE OBLIGATIONS OF FRIENDSHIP, BUT, MOST OF ALL, TO PLEDGE ALLEGIANCE TO THE FRATERNITY WHICH GUIDES US, FROM THIS DAY FORWARD, BE IT OUR SOLE AND SACRED OATH, AMEN.

my dad

AMEN

AMEN

AMEN

HE WAS *RIGHT*

RELEASE

SWIG

SHUT

SET

YANK

NOW, CAN YOU REPEAT WHAT I JUST SAID, VAG?

VAG! *REPEAT* WHAT *I JUST* SAID!

S-SIR, I...I...

brothers,

THIS VAG-**HOLE** THINKS HE CAN BECOME A LAMBDA-DELT WITHOUT **PAYING ATTENTION** TO THE RECITATION OF OUR *SACRED OATH!*

BROTHERS, HE MUST FEEL THE HEAT OF THE *RED HOT LAMBDA-DELT POKER* ON HIS LILY-WHITE FARMBOY ASS TO KNOW WE MEAN *BUSINESS!*

WHAT?

GUYS, WHAT ARE YOU—

OWW!

HA HA HA HA

GUYS! HEY YOU GUYS, WHAT'RE YOU DOING?

now,

C'MON WHAT'S GOING ON, REALLY?

THAT THIS VAG KNOWS WE AREN'T JOKING, HE MUST CHOOSE ONE OF THREE PATHS:

1 *RECITE,* PERFECTLY AND WITHOUT ERROR, THE PLEDGE OF THE LAMBDA-DELTS
   (AS HAVE ALL OUR FATHERS AND BROTHERS...)

2 *SUFFER* THE INTENSE PAIN OF THE RED HOT POKER AS PUNISHMENT
   (AS HAVE ALL OUR FATHERS AND BROTHERS...)

3 OR...

SHOVE THIS TAMPON UP HIS ASS

HA HA HAHA

WHAT'LL IT BE... *VAG?*

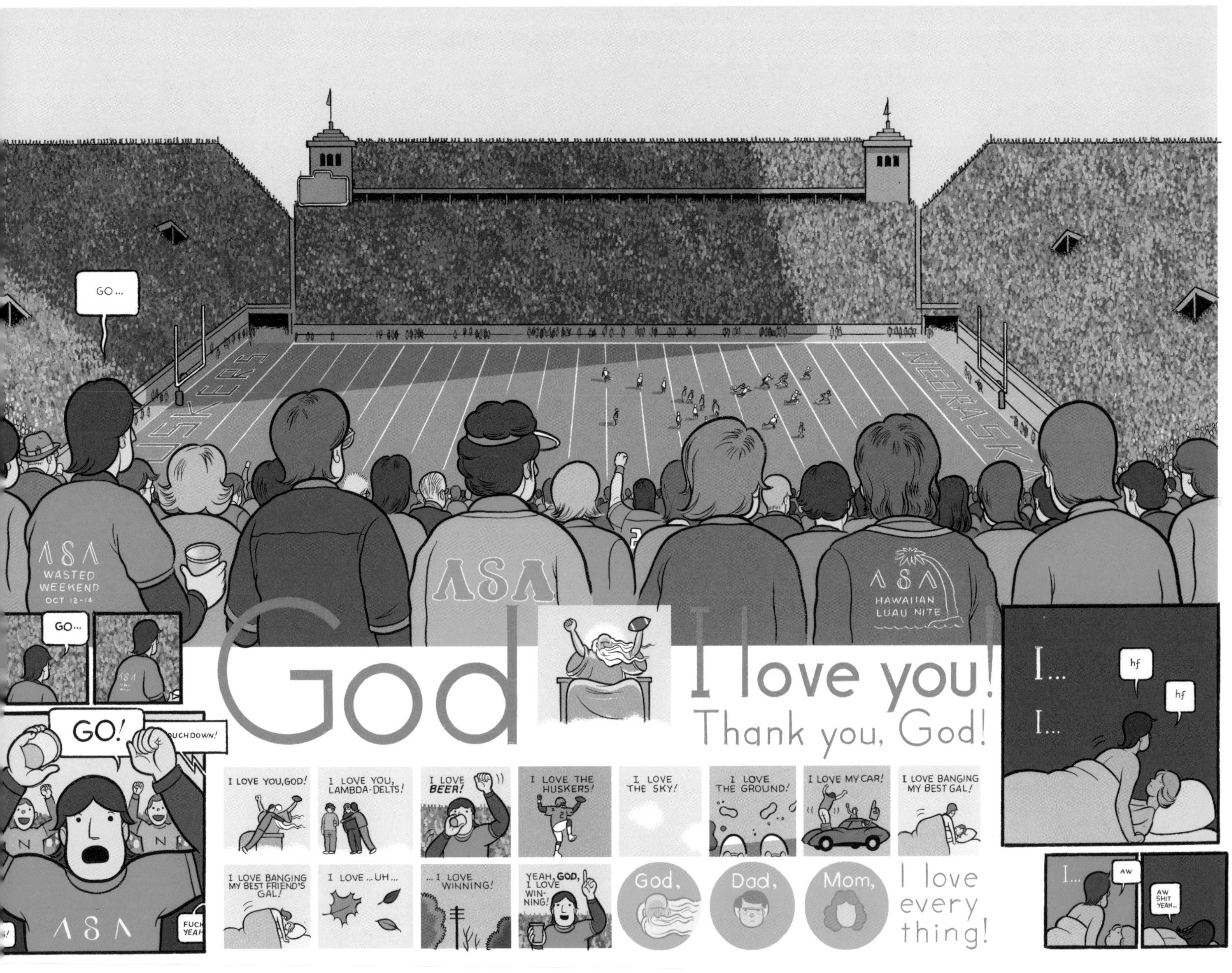
GO...
HUSKERS
NEBRASKA
ΛδΛ
WASTED
WEEKEND
OCT 12-14
ΛδΛ
ΛδΛ
HAWAIIAN
LUAU NITE
GO...
GO!
OUCHDOWN!
ΛδΛ
FUCK
YEAH
God
I love you!
Thank you, God!
I LOVE YOU, GOD!
I LOVE YOU, LAMBDA-DELTS!
I LOVE BEER!
I LOVE THE HUSKERS!
I LOVE THE SKY!
I LOVE THE GROUND!
I LOVE MY CAR!
I LOVE BANGING MY BEST GAL!
I LOVE BANGING MY BEST FRIEND'S GAL!
I LOVE ... UH ...
... I LOVE WINNING!
YEAH, GOD, I LOVE WIN-NING!
God,
Dad,
Mom,
I love every thing!
I...
I...
hf
hf
I...
AW
AW SHIT YEAH...

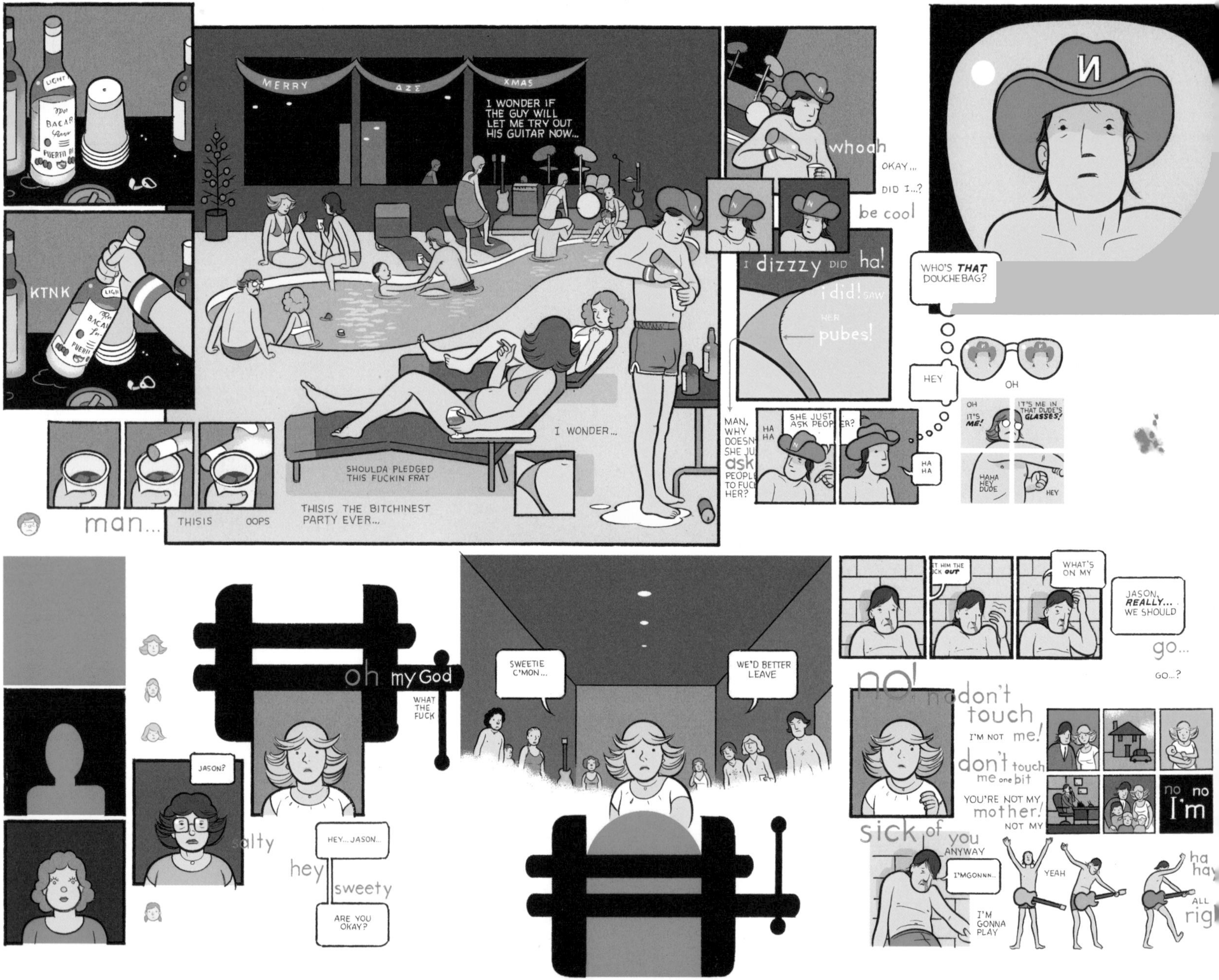
KTNK
MERRY
ΔΖΣ
XMAS
I WONDER IF THE GUY WILL LET ME TRY OUT HIS GUITAR NOW...
I WONDER...
SHOULDA PLEDGED THIS FUCKIN FRAT
THISIS THE BITCHINEST PARTY EVER...
man...
THISIS
OOPS
whoah
OKAY...
DID I...?
be cool
I dizzzy DID ha!
i did! SAW HER pubes!
HA HA
HA HA
WHO'S THAT DOUCHEBAG?
HEY
OH
OH IT'S ME!
IT'S ME IN THAT DUDE'S GLASSES!
HAHA HEY DUDE
HEY
oh my God
WHAT THE FUCK
JASON?
salty
hey
sweety
HEY... JASON...
ARE YOU OKAY?
SWEETIE C'MON...
WE'D BETTER LEAVE
WHAT'S ON MY
JASON, REALLY... WE SHOULD
go...
GO...?
no! no don't touch
I'M NOT me!
don't touch me one bit
YOU'RE NOT MY mother!
NOT MY
no no I'm
sick of you
ANYWAY
I'MGONNN...
I'M GONNA PLAY
YEAH
ha ha
ALL rig

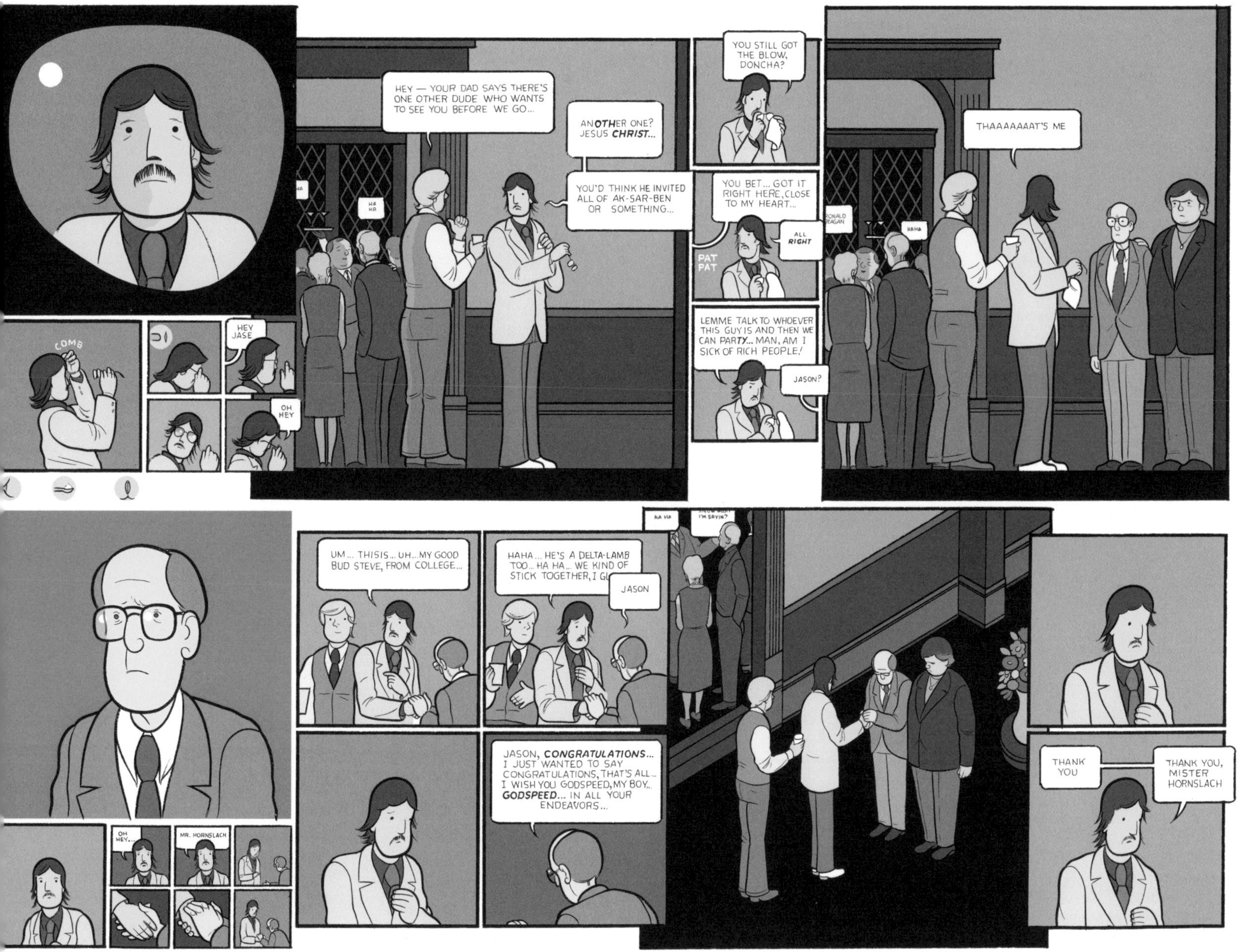
COMB
HEY JASE
OH HEY
HEY — YOUR DAD SAYS THERE'S ONE OTHER DUDE WHO WANTS TO SEE YOU BEFORE WE GO...
ANOTHER ONE? JESUS **CHRIST...**
YOU'D THINK HE INVITED ALL OF AK-SAR-BEN OR SOMETHING...
HA HA
YOU STILL GOT THE BLOW, DONCHA?
YOU BET... GOT IT RIGHT HERE, CLOSE TO MY HEART...
ALL **RIGHT**
PAT PAT
LEMME TALK TO WHOEVER THIS GUY IS AND THEN WE CAN PAR*TY*... MAN, AM I SICK OF RICH PEOPLE!
JASON?
THAAAAAAAT'S ME
RONALD REAGAN
HAHA
OH HEY...
MR. HORNSLACH
UM... THIS IS... UH... MY GOOD BUD STEVE, FROM COLLEGE...
HAHA... HE'S A DELTA-LAMB TOO... HA HA... WE KIND OF STICK TOGETHER, I GU
JASON
JASON, **CONGRATULATIONS...** I JUST WANTED TO SAY CONGRATULATIONS, THAT'S ALL... I WISH YOU GODSPEED, MY BOY... **GODSPEED...** IN ALL YOUR ENDEAVORS...
HA HA
THANK YOU
THANK YOU, MISTER HORNSLACH

hh hh hh
OH MAN OH YEAH OH YEAH
OH MAN YOU'RE GONNA MAKE ME CUM **AGAIN,** BABE
OH YEAH
OH SHIT
oh
YEAH
OH FUCK
OH
OH
oh God
ARE YOU HAPPY WITH THAT OR D'YOU WANNA PUNCH IT IN AGAIN?
OH MAN...
OH MAN THEY SHOULD ***LEAVE*** IT... I THINK IT FUCKING ***ROCKED***
okay WELL dude... ex cuuse me then, fuck you, okay? fuck you
Y'KNOW I'm THE GUY PAYING YOUR FUCKING HOURLY RATE man ($95 × 10 = $950 + TAPE $25 + uh $45 usage fee... is... um... a lot...)
but Y'KNOW I can too! I'm not JUST SOME FUCKIN loser
Y'KNOW? I'm not JUST SOME FUCKIN money man
YOU JUST WAIT AND SEE, OKAY? Mister 'Hotel California'...
okay, dude?
I DIDN'T MOVE HERE TO BE insulted, okay?
you just wait... YOU JUST wait...: WHEN THIS HITS STORES & SOARS TO #1 AND IT'S all over MTV... then ARE YOU GONNA SNUB ME asswipe?
MAYBE A LITTLE LESS PREVERB ON THE SNARE, THOUGH
UH... LET
KEEP IT A
OKAY
kof
dude, hello
I'M TALKI
TO YOU
'SCUSE ME
ROCK
PREVERB? HELLO?
okay...
ROLL
hhhKT
hhhKT
THERE... WHADDYA THINK?
HUH? ARE YOU TALKING TO ME?
hhhKT
YEAH... I CUT THE PREVERB LIKE YOU SAID... IS IT OKAY?
hhhKT
SOUNDS BETTER TO ***ME***
DONCHA THINK?
YEAH...
snf
YEA
AWES

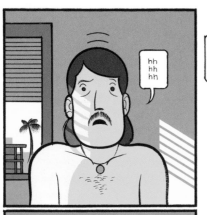

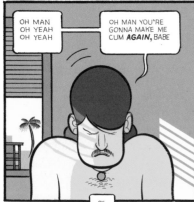

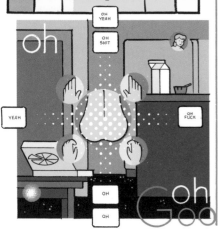

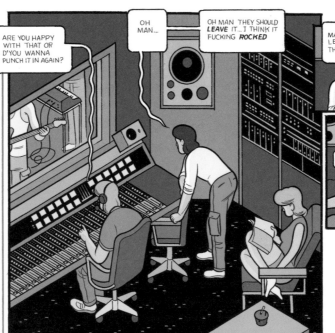

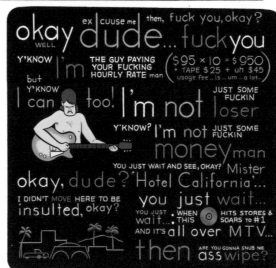

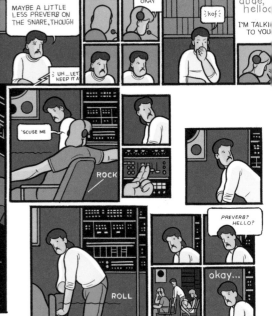

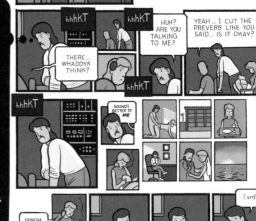

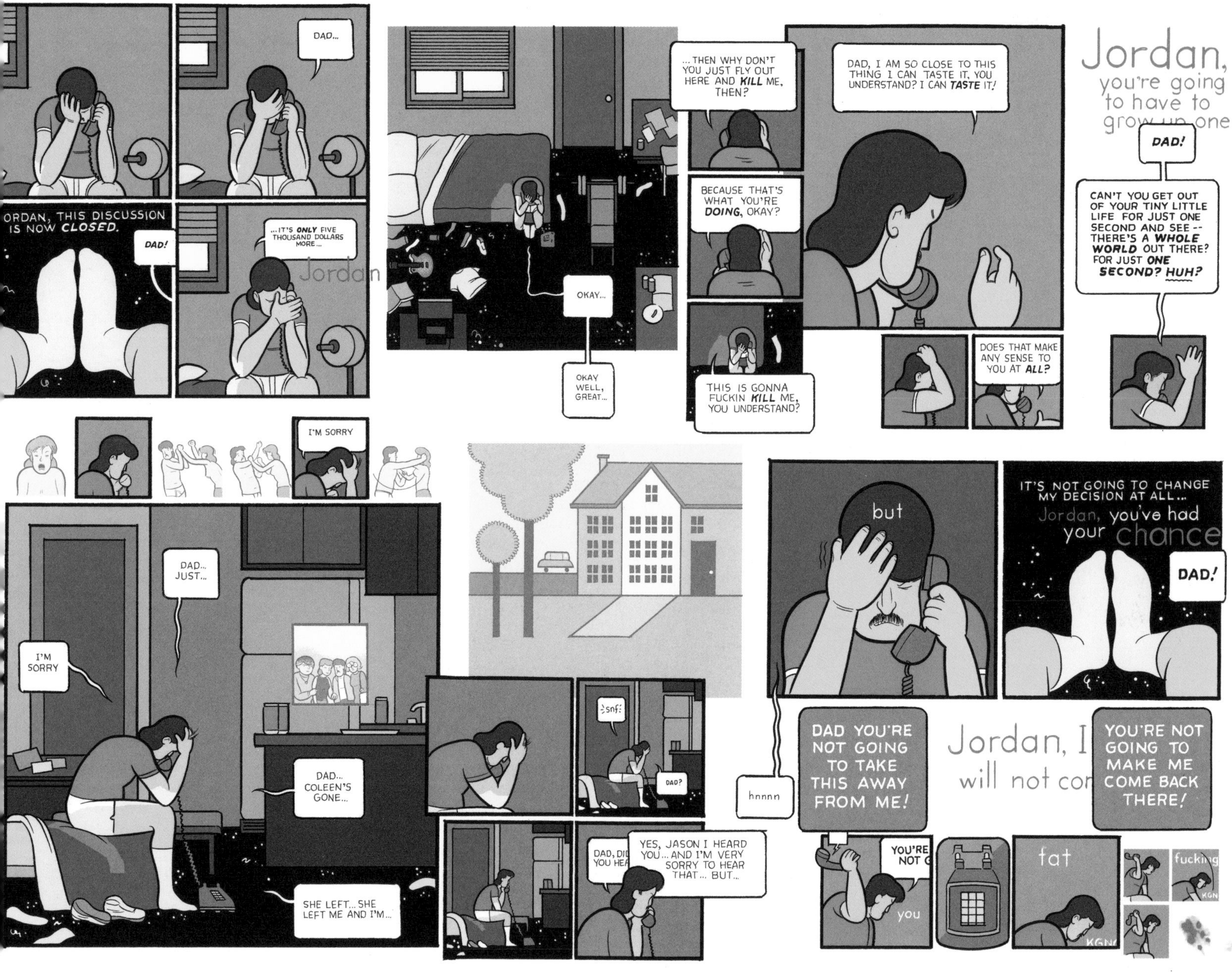
DAD...
ORDAN, THIS DISCUSSION IS NOW CLOSED.
DAD!
...IT'S ONLY FIVE THOUSAND DOLLARS MORE...
Jordan
OKAY...
OKAY WELL, GREAT...
...THEN WHY DON'T YOU JUST FLY OUT HERE AND KILL ME, THEN?
BECAUSE THAT'S WHAT YOU'RE DOING, OKAY?
THIS IS GONNA FUCKIN KILL ME, YOU UNDERSTAND?
DAD, I AM SO CLOSE TO THIS THING I CAN TASTE IT, YOU UNDERSTAND? I CAN TASTE IT!
DOES THAT MAKE ANY SENSE TO YOU AT ALL?
Jordan, you're going to have to grow up one
DAD!
CAN'T YOU GET OUT OF YOUR TINY LITTLE LIFE FOR JUST ONE SECOND AND SEE -- THERE'S A WHOLE WORLD OUT THERE? FOR JUST ONE SECOND? HUH?
I'M SORRY
DAD... JUST...
I'M SORRY
DAD... COLEEN'S GONE...
SHE LEFT... SHE LEFT ME AND I'M...
snf
DAD?
DAD, DID YOU HEA
YES, JASON I HEARD YOU... AND I'M VERY SORRY TO HEAR THAT... BUT...
but
IT'S NOT GOING TO CHANGE MY DECISION AT ALL...
Jordan, you've had your chance
DAD!
hnnnn
DAD YOU'RE NOT GOING TO TAKE THIS AWAY FROM ME!
Jordan, I will not co
YOU'RE NOT GOING TO MAKE ME COME BACK THERE!
YOU'RE NOT G
you
fat
fucking

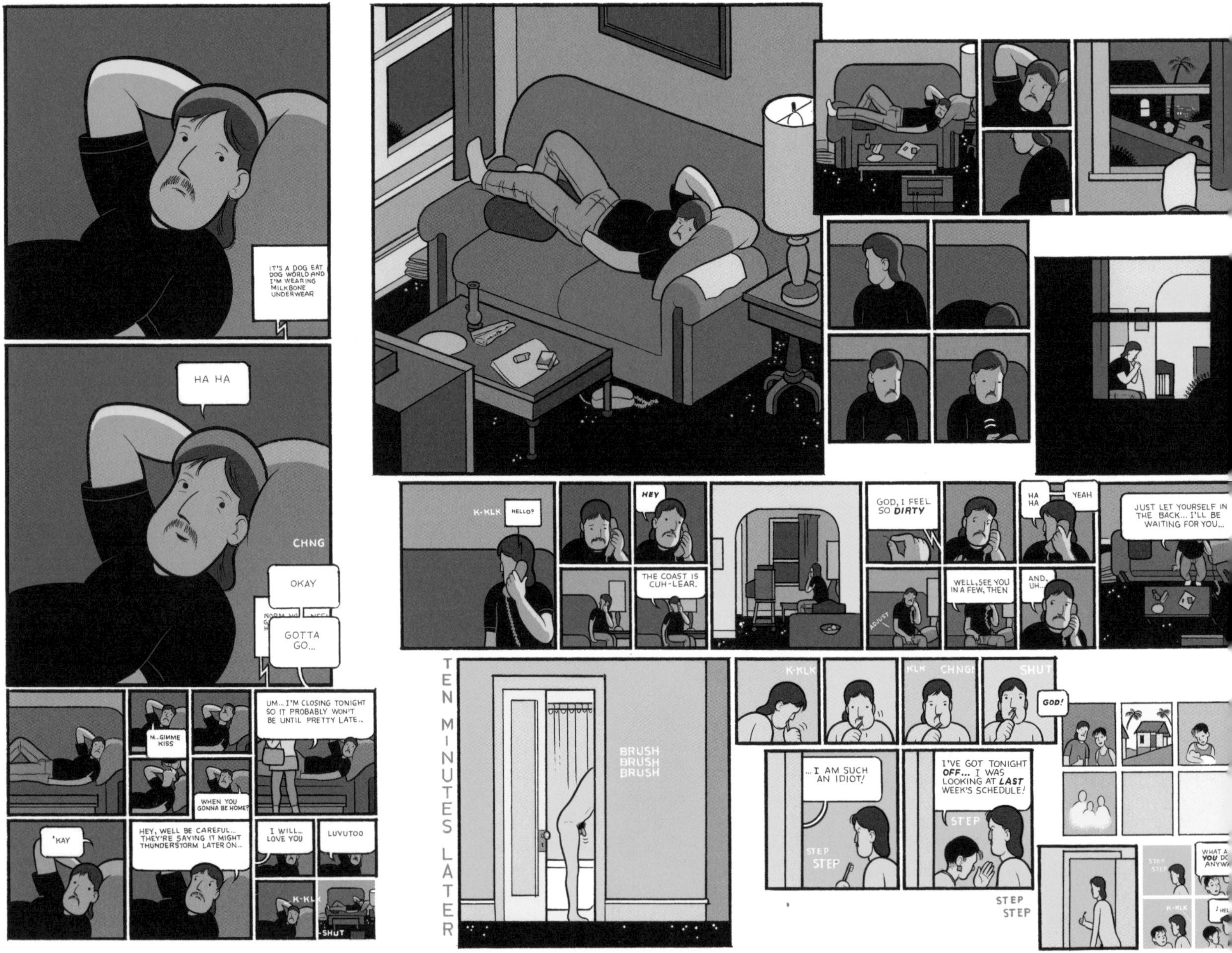

IT'S A DOG EAT DOG WORLD AND I'M WEARING MILKBONE UNDERWEAR
HA HA
CHNG
OKAY
GOTTA GO...
M...GIMME KISS
WHEN YOU GONNA BE HOME?
UM... I'M CLOSING TONIGHT SO IT PROBABLY WON'T BE UNTIL PRETTY LATE...
'KAY
HEY, WELL BE CAREFUL... THEY'RE SAYING IT MIGHT THUNDERSTORM LATER ON...
I WILL... LOVE YOU
LUVUTOO
K-KLK
SHUT
K-KLK
HELLO?
HEY
THE COAST IS CUH-LEAR.
GOD, I FEEL SO DIRTY
ADJUST
HA HA
YEAH
WELL, SEE YOU IN A FEW, THEN
AND, UH...
JUST LET YOURSELF IN THE BACK... I'LL BE WAITING FOR YOU...
TEN MINUTES LATER
BRUSH BRUSH BRUSH
K-KLK
KLK
CHNG!
SHUT
GOD!
... I AM SUCH AN IDIOT!
STEP STEP
I'VE GOT TONIGHT OFF... I WAS LOOKING AT LAST WEEK'S SCHEDULE!
STEP
STEP STEP
K-KLK

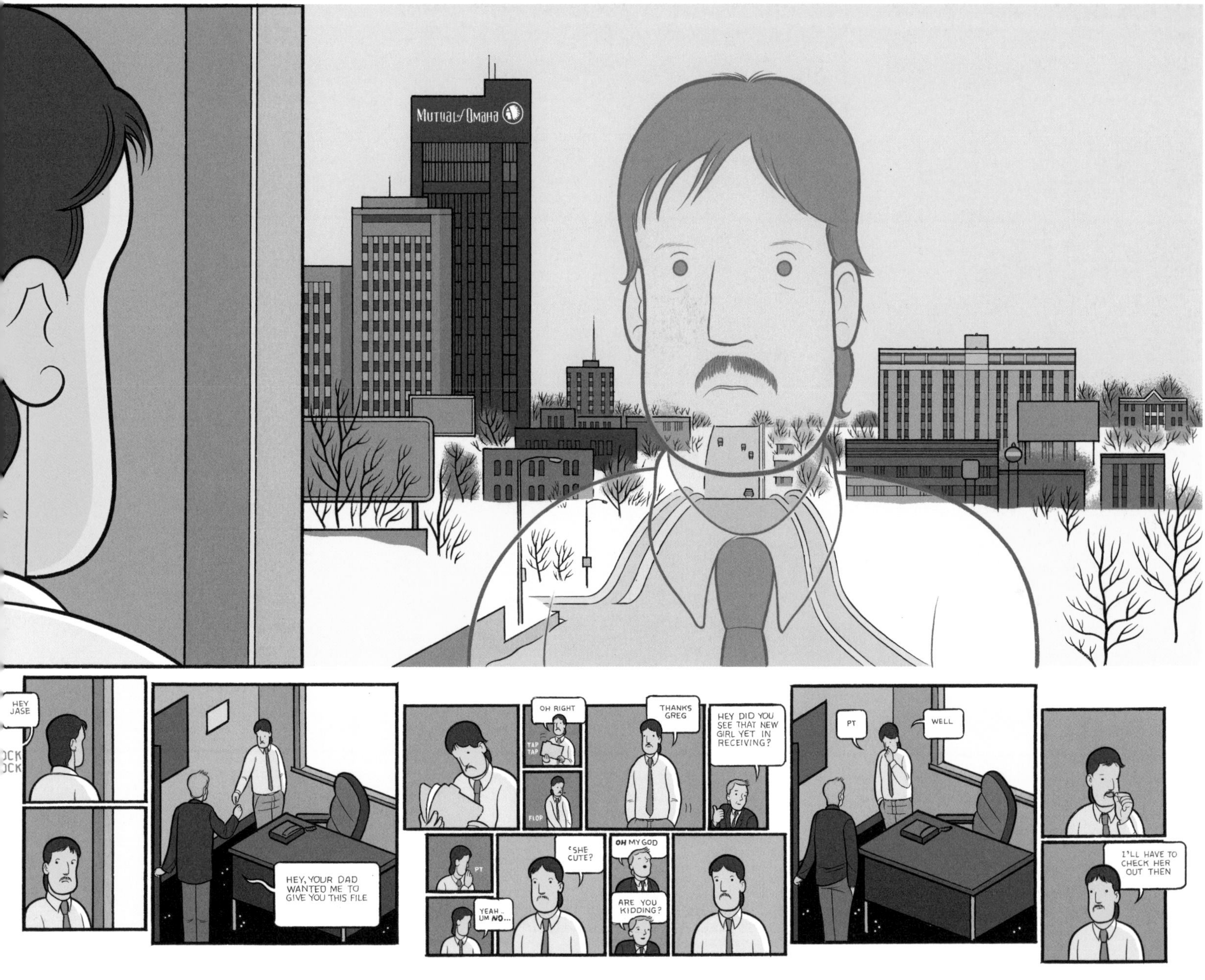
MUTUAL of OMAHA
HEY JASE
HEY, YOUR DAD WANTED ME TO GIVE YOU THIS FILE
OH RIGHT
TAP TAP
FLOP
THANKS GREG
HEY DID YOU SEE THAT NEW GIRL YET IN RECEIVING?
PT
YEAH.. UM NO...
'SHE CUTE?
OH MY GOD
ARE YOU KIDDING?
PT
WELL
I'LL HAVE TO CHECK HER OUT THEN

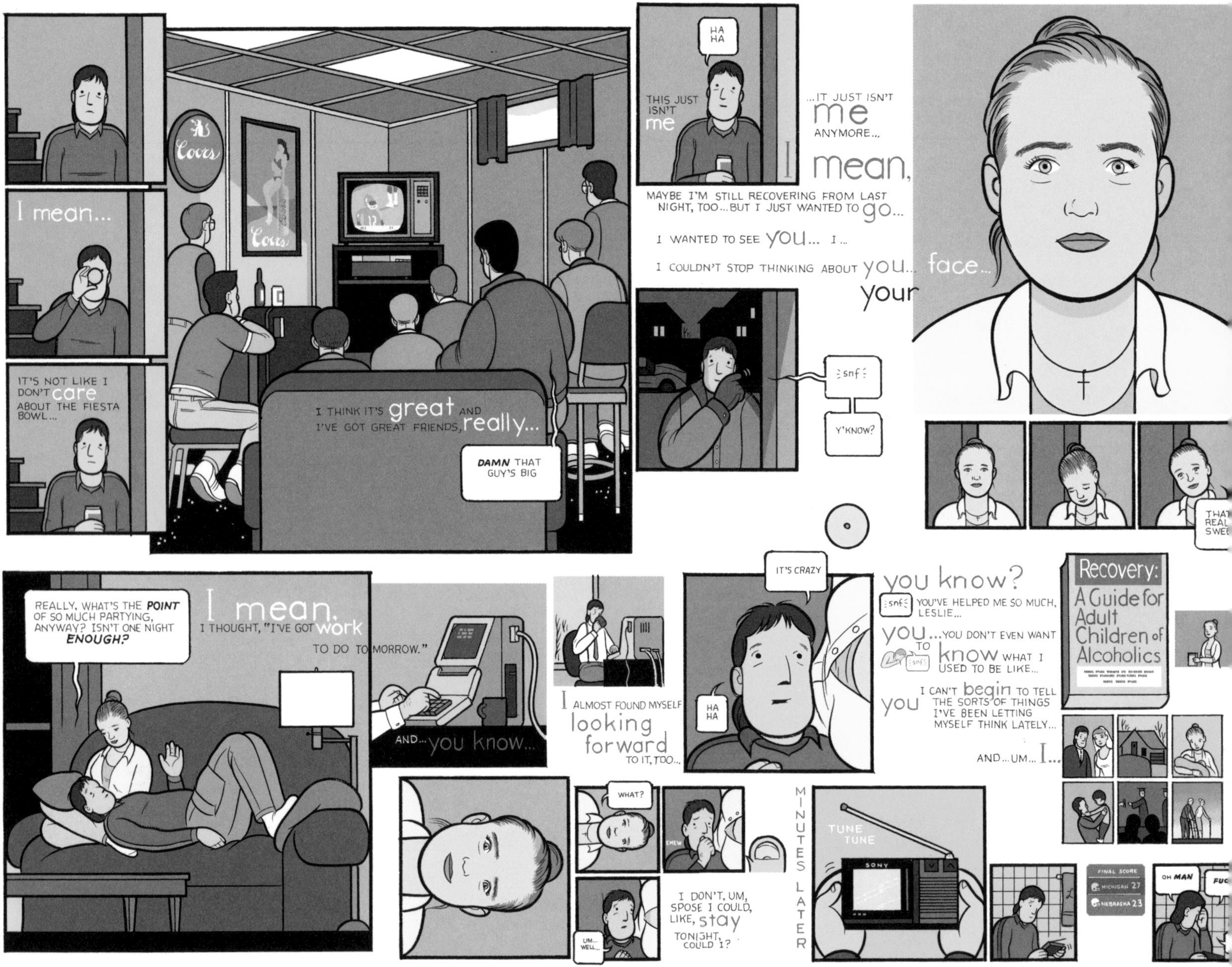
I mean...
IT'S NOT LIKE I DON'T care ABOUT THE FIESTA BOWL...
I THINK IT'S great AND I'VE GOT GREAT FRIENDS, really...
DAMN THAT GUY'S BIG
HA HA
THIS JUST ISN'T me
...IT JUST ISN'T me ANYMORE...
I mean,
MAYBE I'M STILL RECOVERING FROM LAST NIGHT, TOO... BUT I JUST WANTED TO go...
I WANTED TO SEE you... I...
I COULDN'T STOP THINKING ABOUT you... your face...
snf
Y'KNOW?
THAT REAL SWEE
REALLY, WHAT'S THE POINT OF SO MUCH PARTYING, ANYWAY? ISN'T ONE NIGHT ENOUGH?
I mean, I THOUGHT, "I'VE GOT work TO DO TOMORROW."
AND... you know...
I ALMOST FOUND MYSELF looking forward TO IT, TOO...
IT'S CRAZY
HA HA
you know?
snf
YOU'VE HELPED ME SO MUCH, LESLIE...
you... YOU DON'T EVEN WANT TO know WHAT I USED TO BE LIKE...
snf
you I CAN'T begin TO TELL THE SORTS OF THINGS I'VE BEEN LETTING MYSELF THINK LATELY...
Recovery: A Guide for Adult Children of Alcoholics
AND... UM... I...
WHAT?
CHEW
UM... WELL...
I DON'T, UM, SPOSE I COULD, LIKE, stay TONIGHT, COULD I?
MINUTES LATER
TUNE TUNE
SONY
FINAL SCORE
MICHIGAN 27
NEBRASKA 23
OH MAN
FUC

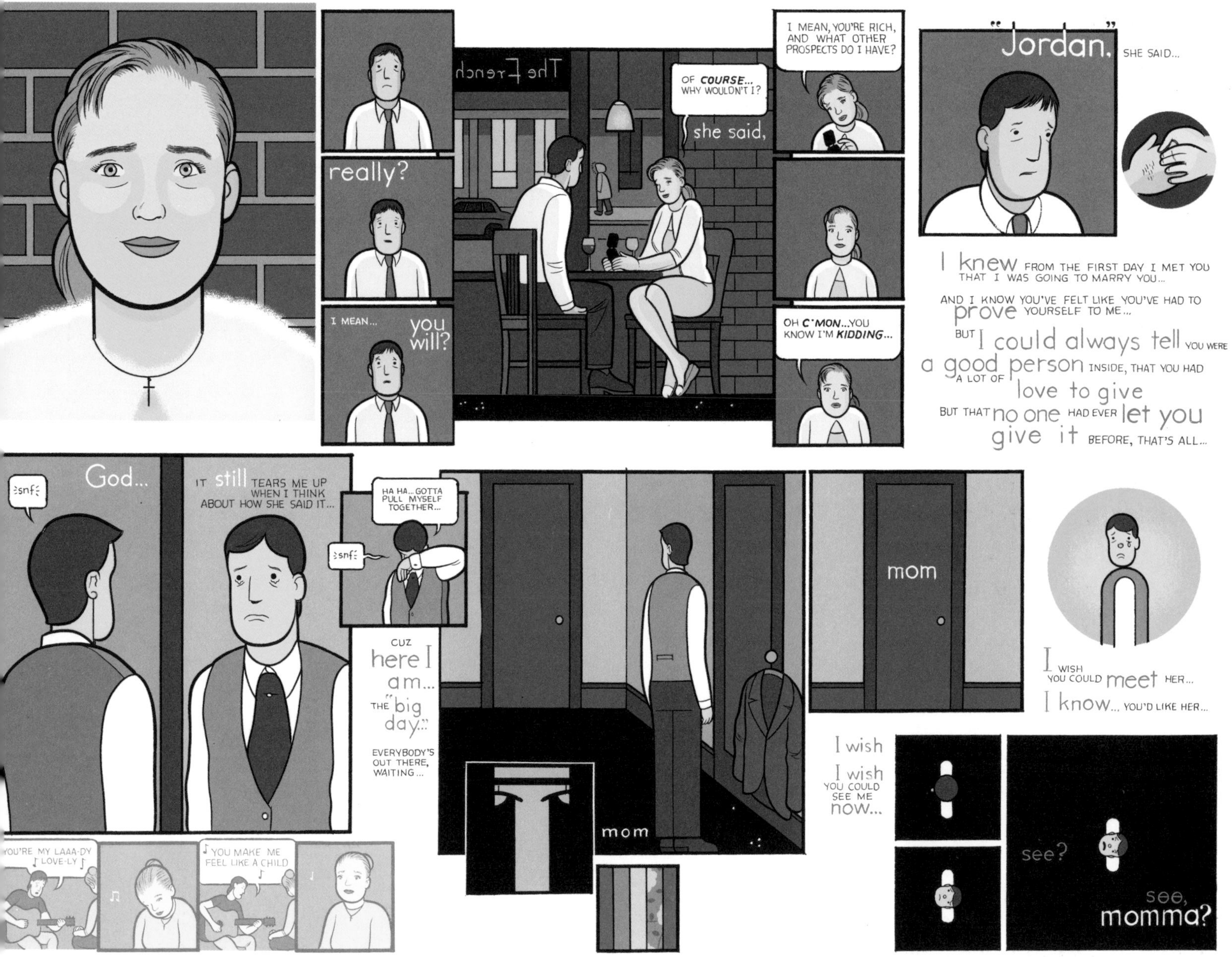
really?
I MEAN... you will?
OF COURSE... WHY WOULDN'T I?
she said,
I MEAN, YOU'RE RICH, AND WHAT OTHER PROSPECTS DO I HAVE?
OH C'MON...YOU KNOW I'M KIDDING...
"Jordan," SHE SAID...
I knew FROM THE FIRST DAY I MET YOU THAT I WAS GOING TO MARRY YOU...
AND I KNOW YOU'VE FELT LIKE YOU'VE HAD TO prove YOURSELF TO ME...
BUT I could always tell YOU WERE a good person INSIDE, THAT YOU HAD A LOT OF love to give
BUT THAT no one HAD EVER let you give it BEFORE, THAT'S ALL...
snf
God...
IT still TEARS ME UP WHEN I THINK ABOUT HOW SHE SAID IT...
HA HA... GOTTA PULL MYSELF TOGETHER...
snf
CUZ here I am... THE "big day."
EVERYBODY'S OUT THERE, WAITING...
mom
mom
I WISH YOU COULD meet HER...
I know... YOU'D LIKE HER...
YOU'RE MY LAAA-DY LOVE-LY
YOU MAKE ME FEEL LIKE A CHILD
I wish
I wish YOU COULD SEE ME now...
see?
see, momma?

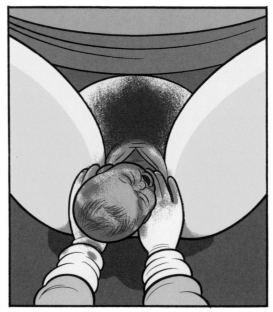

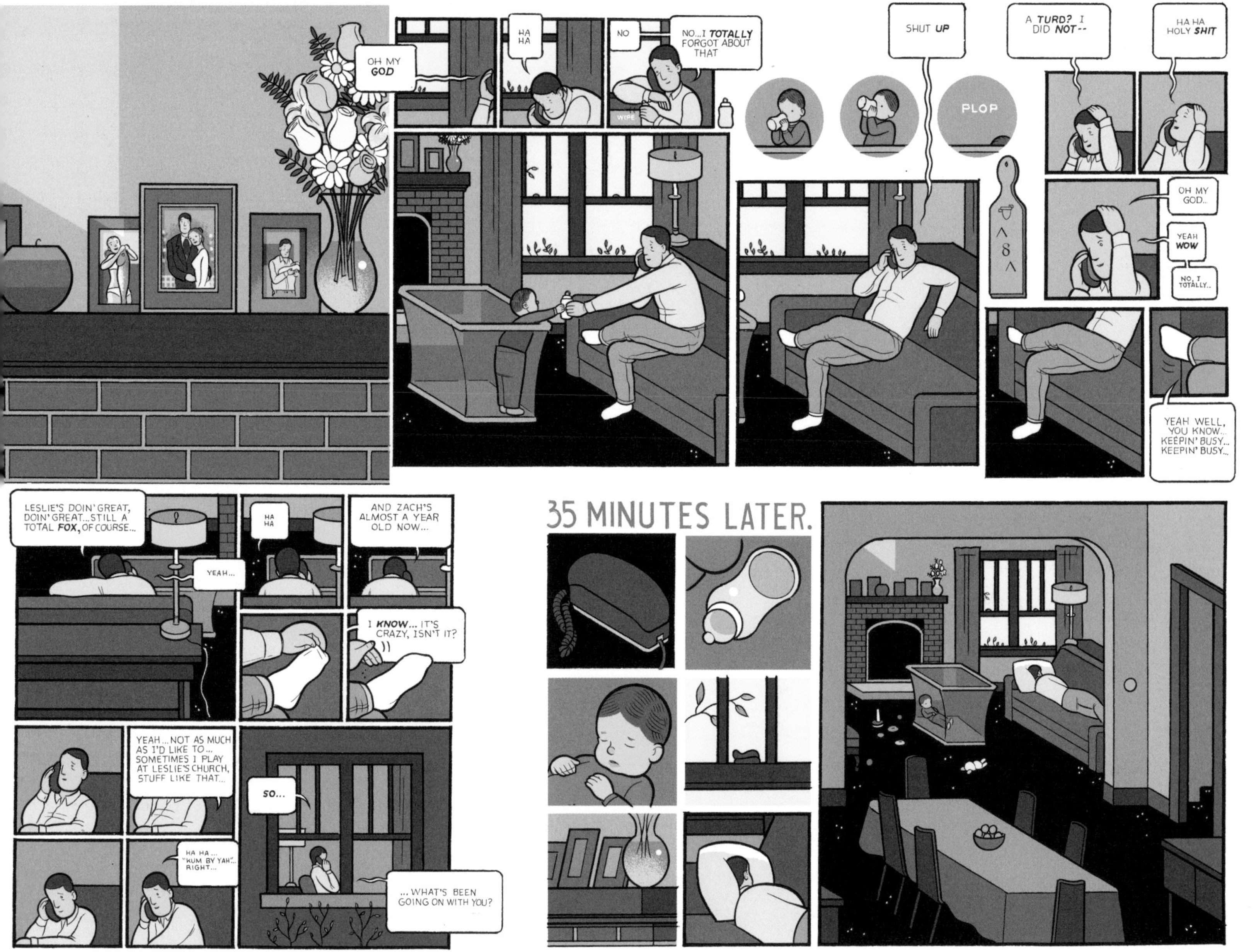

OH MY GOD
HA HA
NO
NO...I TOTALLY FORGOT ABOUT THAT
WIPE
SHUT UP
PLOP
A TURD? I DID NOT--
HA HA HOLY SHIT
OH MY GOD...
YEAH WOW
NO, I TOTALLY..
YEAH WELL, YOU KNOW... KEEPIN' BUSY... KEEPIN' BUSY...
LESLIE'S DOIN' GREAT, DOIN' GREAT...STILL A TOTAL FOX, OF COURSE...
YEAH...
HA HA
AND ZACH'S ALMOST A YEAR OLD NOW...
I KNOW... IT'S CRAZY, ISN'T IT?
YEAH...NOT AS MUCH AS I'D LIKE TO... SOMETIMES I PLAY AT LESLIE'S CHURCH, STUFF LIKE THAT...
SO...
HA HA... "KUM BY YAH"... RIGHT...
...WHAT'S BEEN GOING ON WITH YOU?
35 MINUTES LATER.

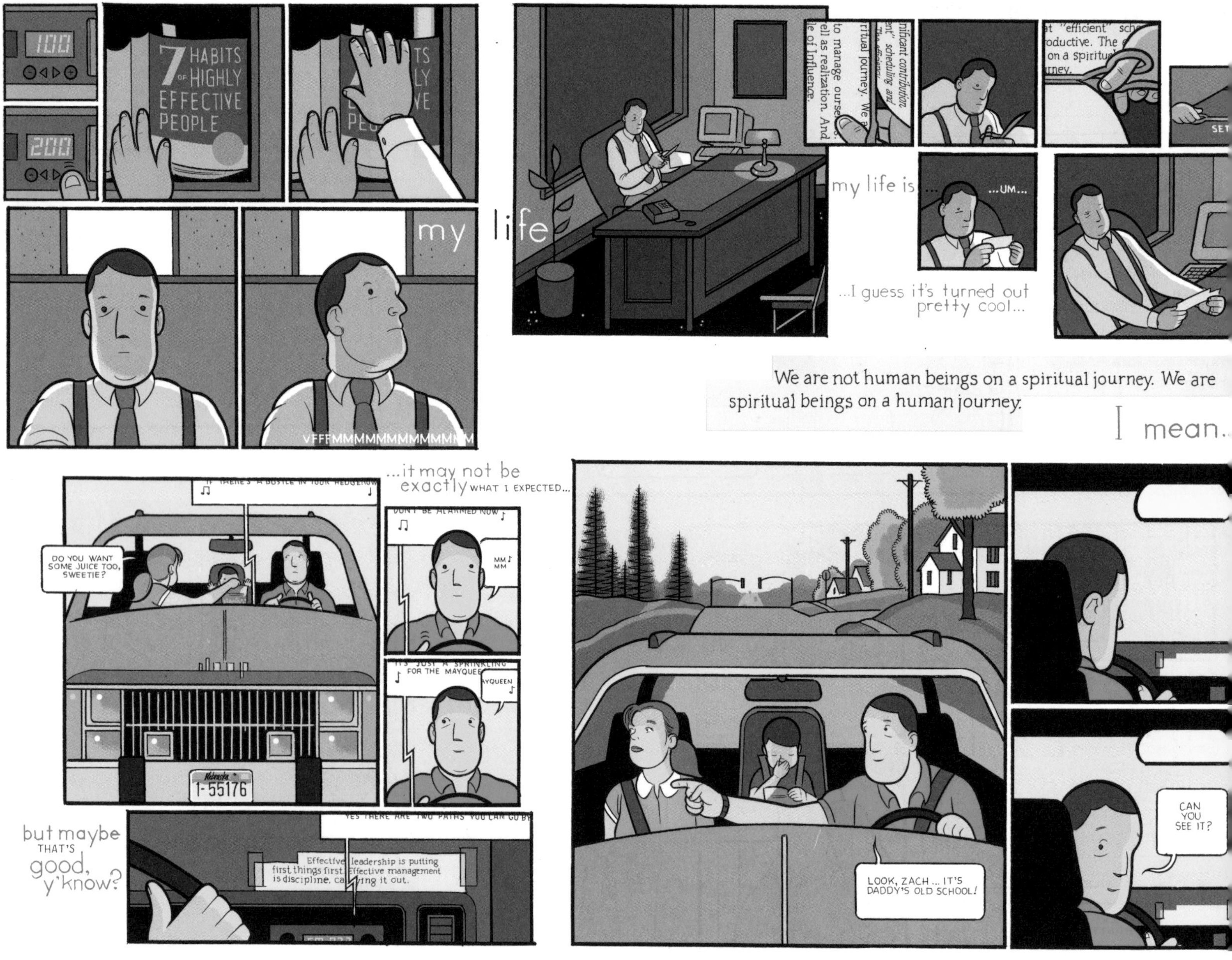

100
200
7 HABITS OF HIGHLY EFFECTIVE PEOPLE
VFFFMMMMMMMMMMMMMM
my life
my life is... ...UM...
...I guess it's turned out pretty cool...
We are not human beings on a spiritual journey. We are spiritual beings on a human journey.
I mean...
...it may not be exactly WHAT I EXPECTED...
DO YOU WANT SOME JUICE TOO, SWEETIE?
MM MM
FOR THE MAYQUEEN
AYQUEEN
1-55176
but maybe THAT'S good, y'know?
Effective leadership is putting first things first. Effective management is discipline, carrying it out.
LOOK, ZACH ... IT'S DADDY'S OLD SCHOOL!
CAN YOU SEE IT?

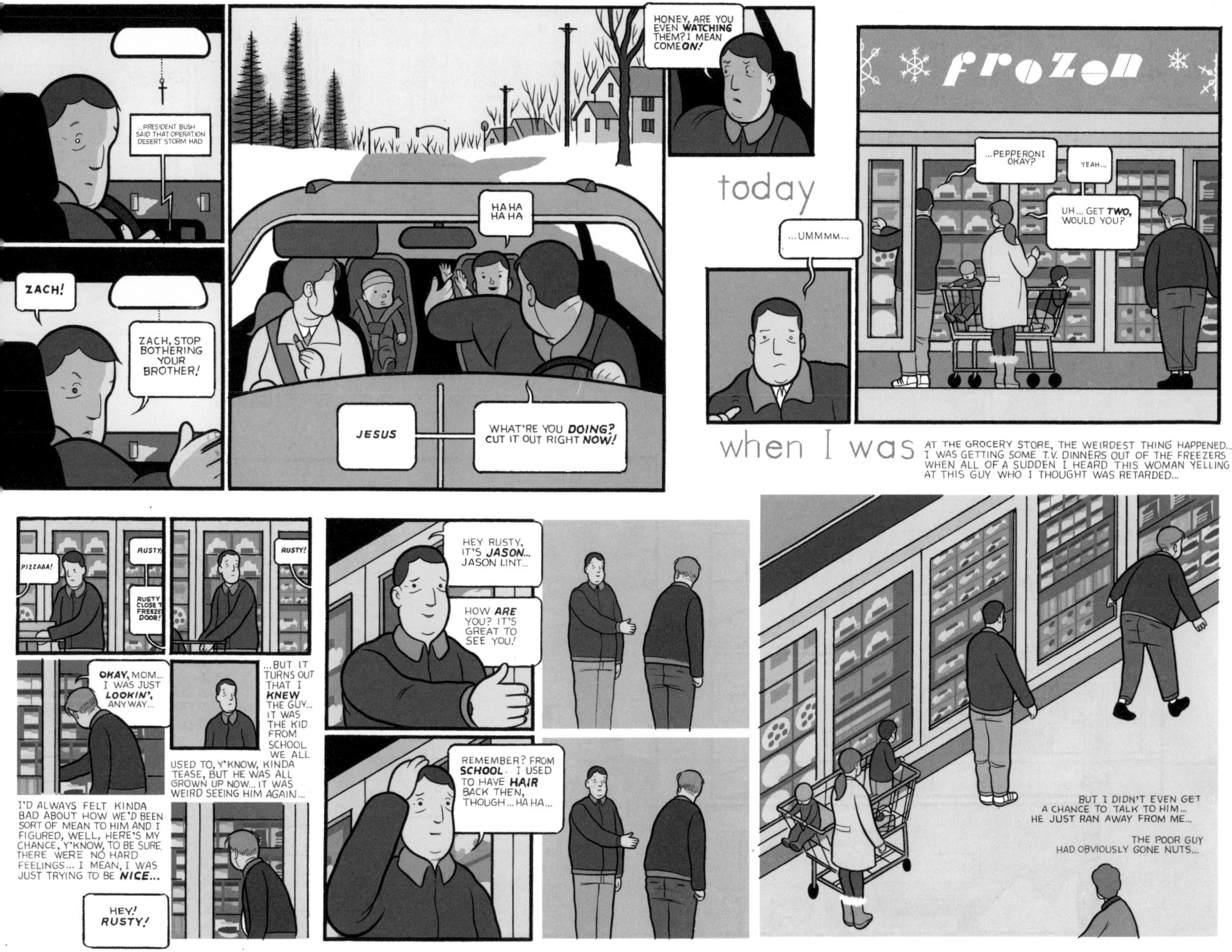
...PRESIDENT BUSH SAID THAT OPERATION DESERT STORM HAD
ZACH!
ZACH, STOP BOTHERING YOUR BROTHER!
HA HA HA HA
JESUS
WHAT'RE YOU DOING? CUT IT OUT RIGHT NOW!
HONEY, ARE YOU EVEN WATCHING THEM? I MEAN COME ON!
today
...UMMMM...
...PEPPERONI OKAY?
YEAH...
UH... GET TWO, WOULD YOU?
frozen
when I was
AT THE GROCERY STORE, THE WEIRDEST THING HAPPENED... I WAS GETTING SOME T.V. DINNERS OUT OF THE FREEZERS WHEN ALL OF A SUDDEN I HEARD THIS WOMAN YELLING AT THIS GUY WHO I THOUGHT WAS RETARDED...
PIZZAAA!
RUSTY
RUSTY CLOSE T FREEZE DOOR!
RUSTY!
OKAY, MOM... I WAS JUST LOOKIN', ANYWAY...
...BUT IT TURNS OUT THAT I KNEW THE GUY... IT WAS THE KID FROM SCHOOL WE ALL USED TO, Y'KNOW, KINDA TEASE, BUT HE WAS ALL GROWN UP NOW... IT WAS WEIRD SEEING HIM AGAIN...
I'D ALWAYS FELT KINDA BAD ABOUT HOW WE'D BEEN SORT OF MEAN TO HIM AND I FIGURED, WELL, HERE'S MY CHANCE, Y'KNOW, TO BE SURE THERE WERE NO HARD FEELINGS... I MEAN, I WAS JUST TRYING TO BE NICE...
HEY! RUSTY!
HEY RUSTY, IT'S JASON... JASON LINT...
HOW ARE YOU? IT'S GREAT TO SEE YOU!
REMEMBER? FROM SCHOOL. I USED TO HAVE HAIR BACK THEN, THOUGH... HA HA...
BUT I DIDN'T EVEN GET A CHANCE TO TALK TO HIM... HE JUST RAN AWAY FROM ME...
THE POOR GUY HAD OBVIOUSLY GONE NUTS...

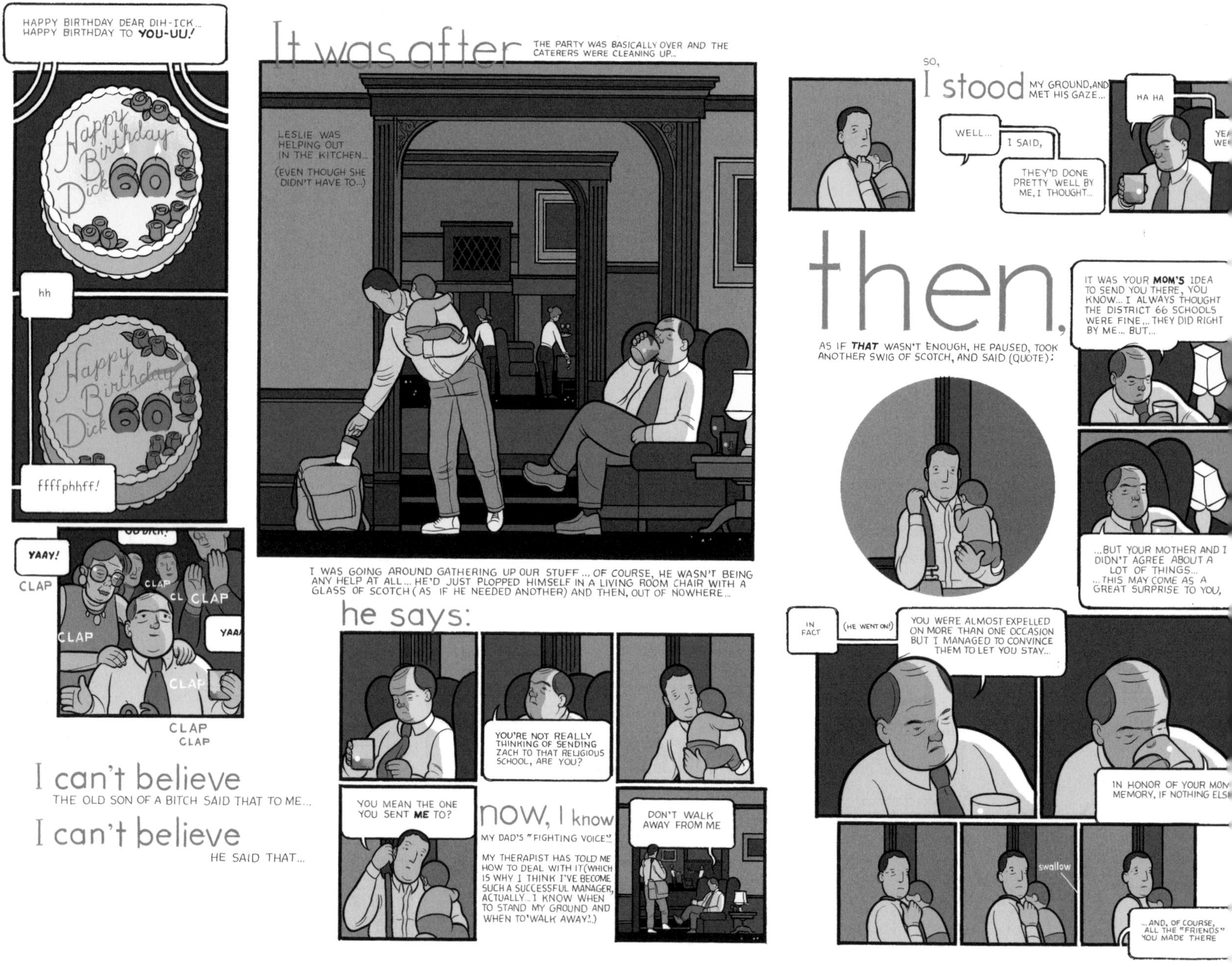

HAPPY BIRTHDAY DEAR DIH-ICK...
HAPPY BIRTHDAY TO **YOU-UU!**
Happy Birthday Dick 60
hh
ffffphhff!
YAAY!
CLAP
CLAP
CL CLAP
CLAP
CLAP
CLAP
CLAP
I can't believe
THE OLD SON OF A BITCH SAID THAT TO ME...
I can't believe
HE SAID THAT...
It was after
THE PARTY WAS BASICALLY OVER AND THE CATERERS WERE CLEANING UP...
LESLIE WAS HELPING OUT IN THE KITCHEN...
(EVEN THOUGH SHE DIDN'T HAVE TO...)
I WAS GOING AROUND GATHERING UP OUR STUFF... OF COURSE, HE WASN'T BEING ANY HELP AT ALL... HE'D JUST PLOPPED HIMSELF IN A LIVING ROOM CHAIR WITH A GLASS OF SCOTCH (AS IF HE NEEDED ANOTHER) AND THEN, OUT OF NOWHERE...
he says:
YOU'RE NOT REALLY THINKING OF SENDING ZACH TO THAT RELIGIOUS SCHOOL, ARE YOU?
YOU MEAN THE ONE YOU SENT **ME** TO?
now, I know
MY DAD'S "FIGHTING VOICE".
MY THERAPIST HAS TOLD ME HOW TO DEAL WITH IT (WHICH IS WHY I THINK I'VE BECOME SUCH A SUCCESSFUL MANAGER, ACTUALLY... I KNOW WHEN TO STAND MY GROUND AND WHEN TO "WALK AWAY".)
DON'T WALK AWAY FROM ME
SO,
I stood
MY GROUND, AND MET HIS GAZE...
WELL...
I SAID,
THEY'D DONE PRETTY WELL BY ME, I THOUGHT...
HA HA
then,
AS IF **THAT** WASN'T ENOUGH, HE PAUSED, TOOK ANOTHER SWIG OF SCOTCH, AND SAID (QUOTE):
IT WAS YOUR **MOM'S** IDEA TO SEND YOU THERE, YOU KNOW... I ALWAYS THOUGHT THE DISTRICT 66 SCHOOLS WERE FINE... THEY DID RIGHT BY ME... BUT...
...BUT YOUR MOTHER AND I DIDN'T AGREE ABOUT A LOT OF THINGS...
...THIS MAY COME AS A GREAT SURPRISE TO YOU,
IN FACT
(HE WENT ON!)
YOU WERE ALMOST EXPELLED ON MORE THAN ONE OCCASION BUT I MANAGED TO CONVINCE THEM TO LET YOU STAY...
IN HONOR OF YOUR MOM MEMORY, IF NOTHING ELS
swallow
...AND, OF COURSE, ALL THE "FRIENDS" YOU MADE THERE

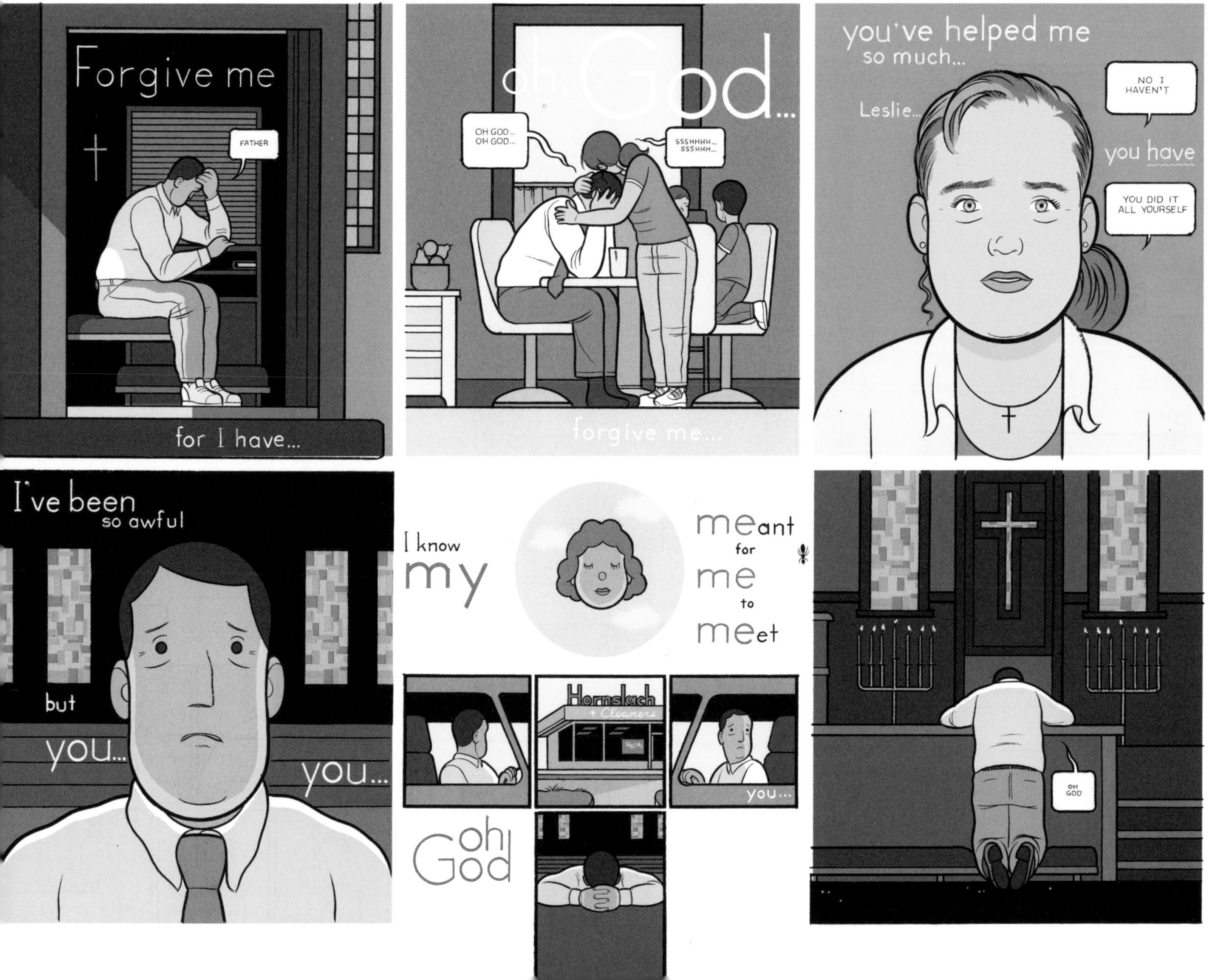
Forgive me
FATHER
for I have...
oh, God...
OH GOD... OH GOD...
SSSHHHH... SSSHHH...
forgive me...
you've helped me so much...
Leslie...
NO I HAVEN'T
you have
YOU DID IT ALL YOURSELF
I've been so awful
but
you...
you...
I know my
meant for me to meet
Hornslech + Cleaners
SPECIAL
you...
oh God
OH GOD

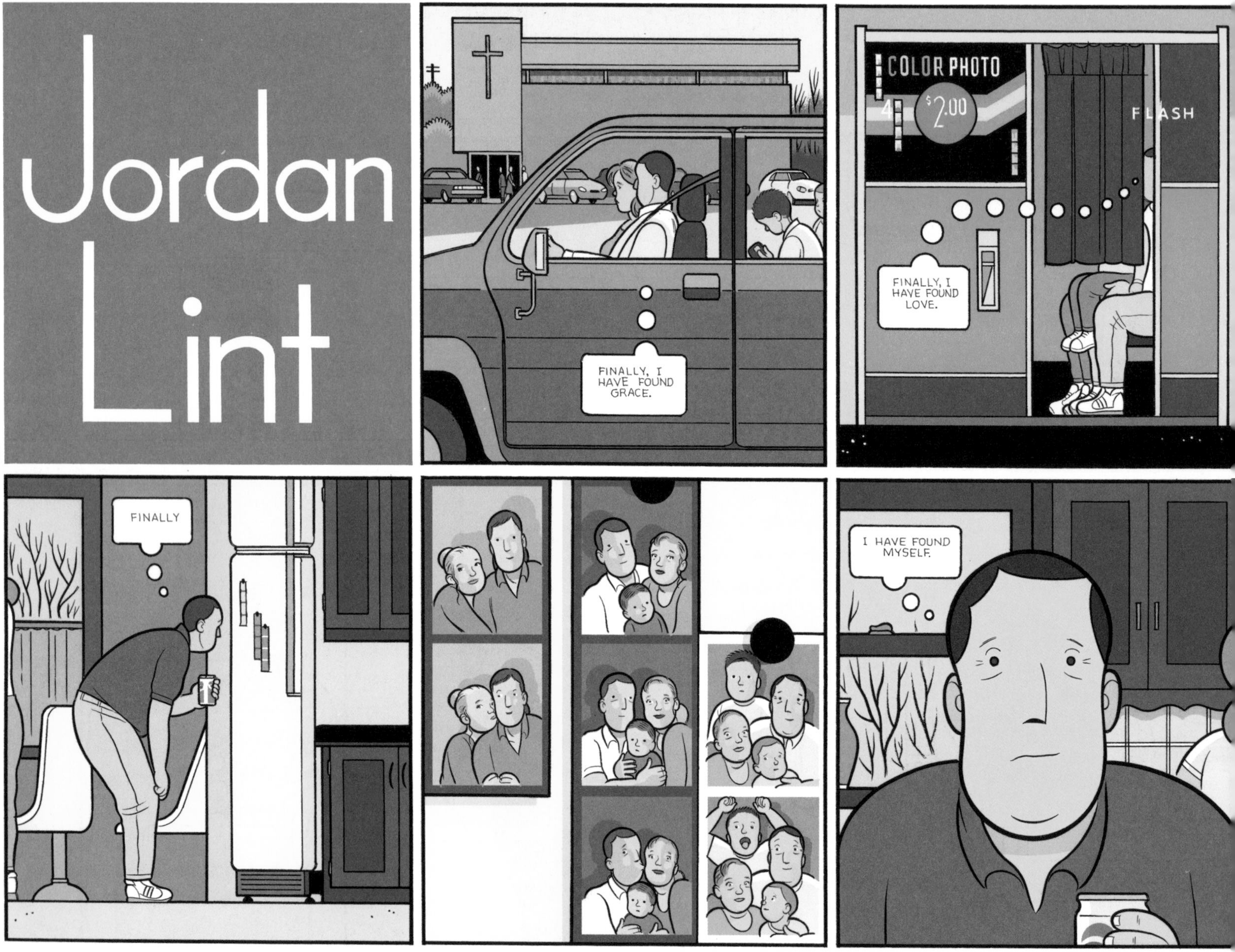
Jordan Lint
FINALLY, I HAVE FOUND GRACE.
COLOR PHOTO
4
$2.00
FLASH
FINALLY, I HAVE FOUND LOVE.
FINALLY
I HAVE FOUND MYSELF.

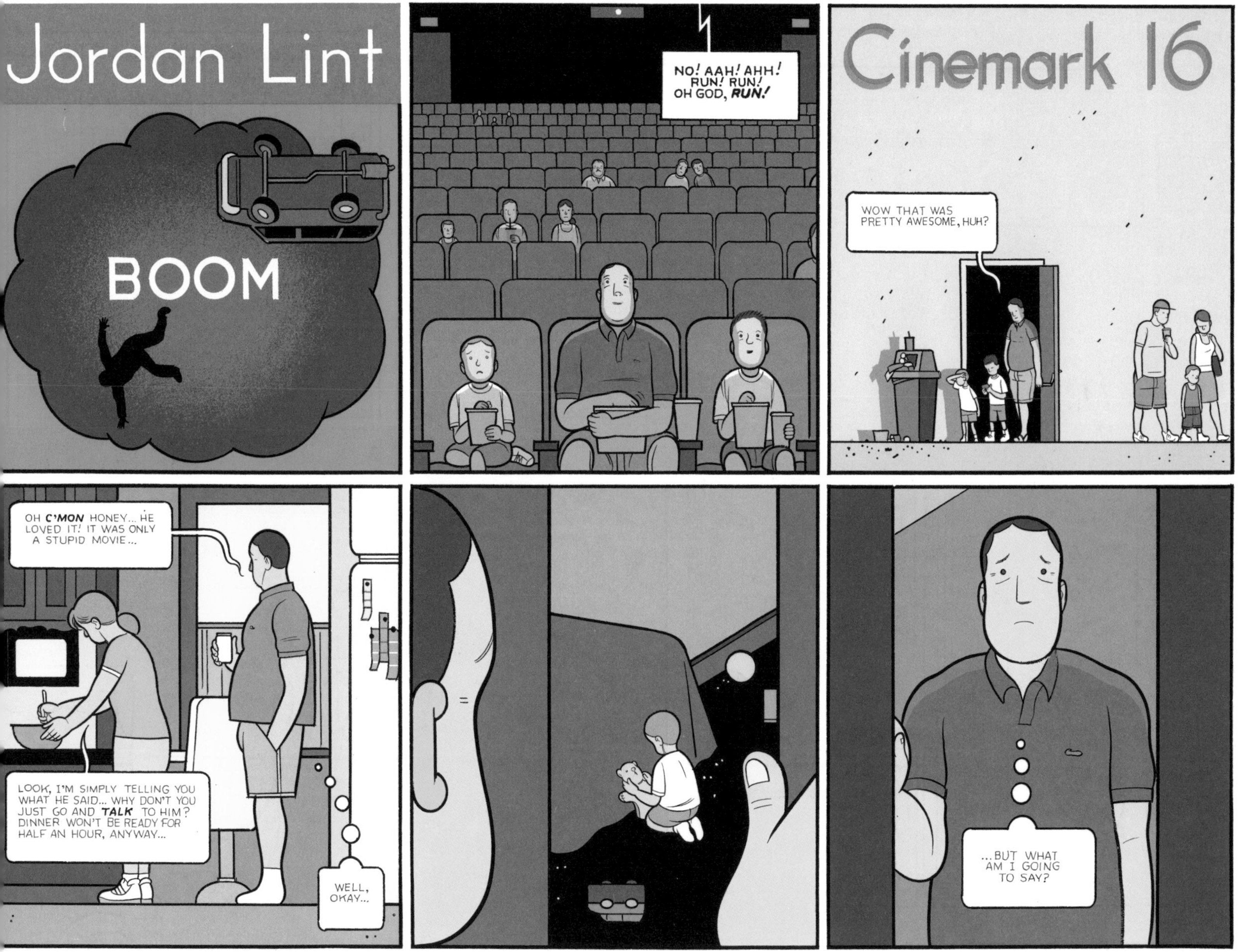

Jordan Lint
BOOM
NO! AAH! AHH! RUN! RUN! OH GOD, **RUN!**
Cinemark 16
WOW THAT WAS PRETTY AWESOME, HUH?
OH **C'MON** HONEY... HE LOVED IT! IT WAS ONLY A STUPID MOVIE...
LOOK, I'M SIMPLY TELLING YOU WHAT HE SAID... WHY DON'T YOU JUST GO AND **TALK** TO HIM? DINNER WON'T BE READY FOR HALF AN HOUR, ANYWAY...
WELL, OKAY...
...BUT WHAT AM I GOING TO SAY?

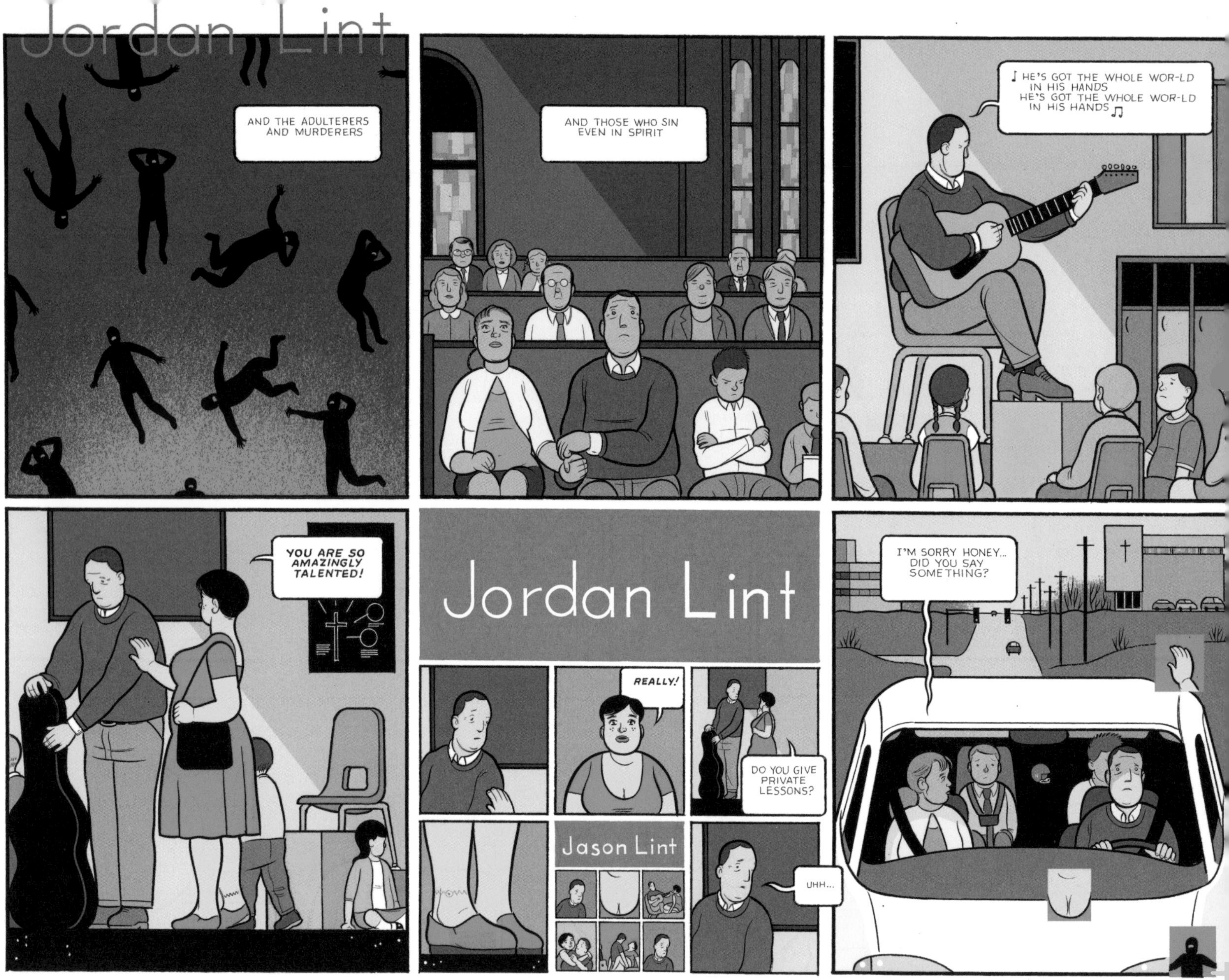

Jordan Lint
AND THE ADULTERERS AND MURDERERS
AND THOSE WHO SIN EVEN IN SPIRIT
HE'S GOT THE WHOLE WOR-LD IN HIS HANDS HE'S GOT THE WHOLE WOR-LD IN HIS HANDS
YOU ARE SO AMAZINGLY TALENTED!
Jordan Lint
REALLY!
DO YOU GIVE PRIVATE LESSONS?
Jason Lint
UHH...
I'M SORRY HONEY... DID YOU SAY SOMETHING?

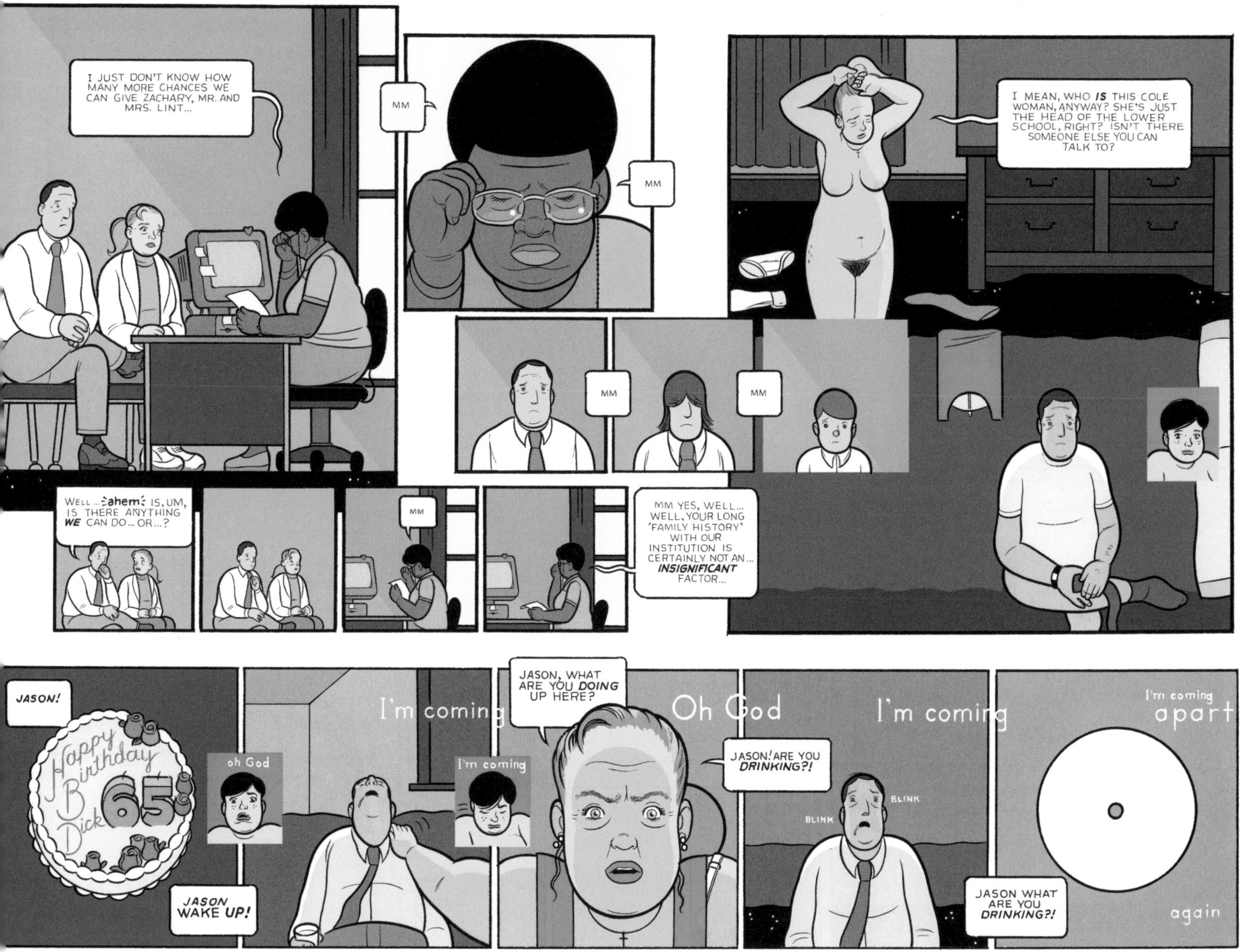
I JUST DON'T KNOW HOW MANY MORE CHANCES WE CAN GIVE ZACHARY, MR. AND MRS. LINT...
MM
MM
I MEAN, WHO IS THIS COLE WOMAN, ANYWAY? SHE'S JUST THE HEAD OF THE LOWER SCHOOL, RIGHT? ISN'T THERE SOMEONE ELSE YOU CAN TALK TO?
MM
MM
WELL... ahem IS, UM, IS THERE ANYTHING WE CAN DO... OR...?
MM
MM YES, WELL... WELL, YOUR LONG 'FAMILY HISTORY' WITH OUR INSTITUTION IS CERTAINLY NOT AN... INSIGNIFICANT FACTOR...
JASON!
Happy Birthday
Dick
65
oh God
JASON WAKE UP!
I'm coming
I'm coming
JASON, WHAT ARE YOU DOING UP HERE?
Oh God
JASON! ARE YOU DRINKING?!
I'm coming
BLINK
BLINK
JASON WHAT ARE YOU DRINKING?!
I'm coming
apart
again

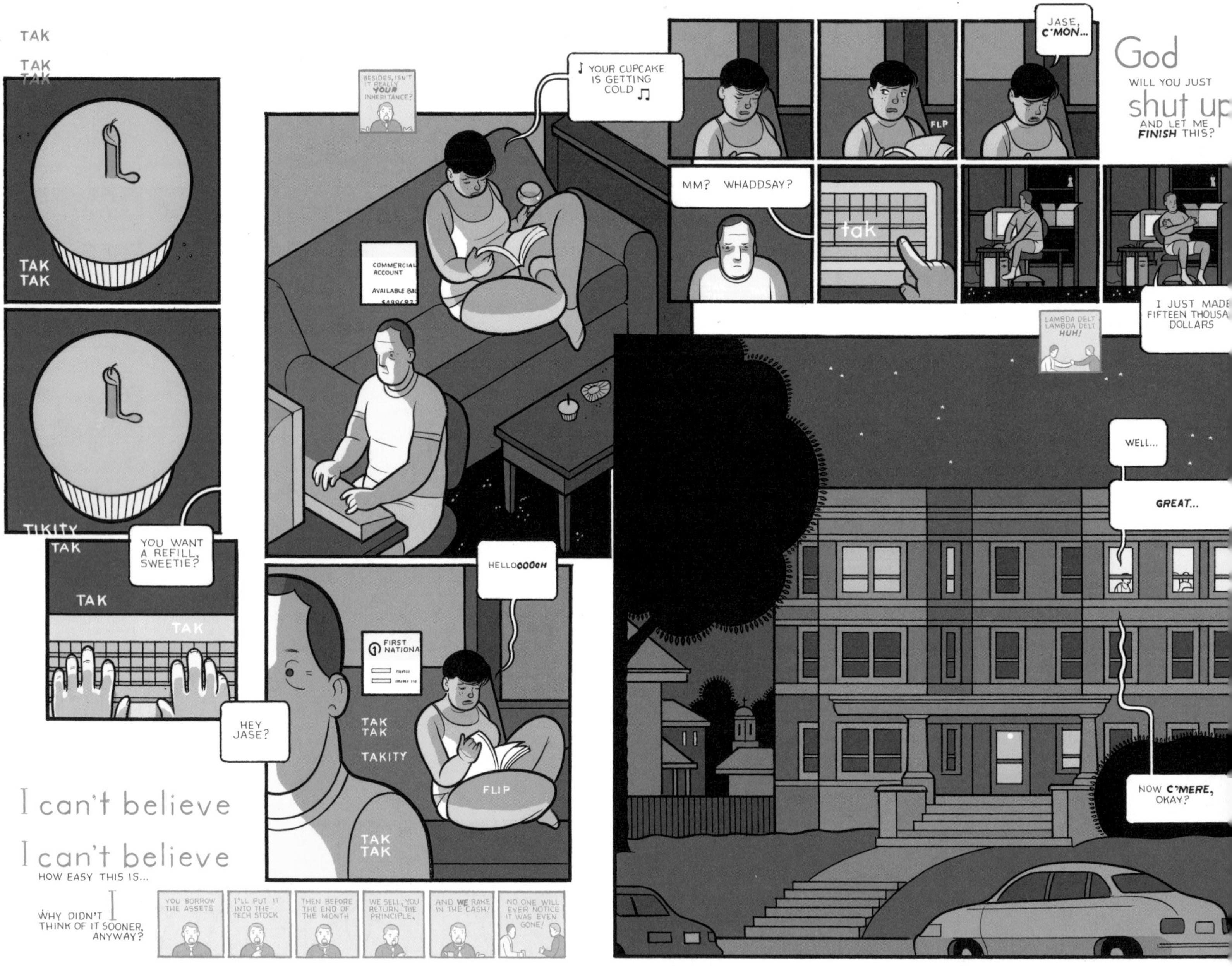

TAK
TAK TAK
TAK TAK
TIKITY TAK
YOU WANT A REFILL, SWEETIE?
TAK
TAK
HEY JASE?
I can't believe
I can't believe
HOW EASY THIS IS...
WHY DIDN'T I THINK OF IT SOONER, ANYWAY?
YOU BORROW THE ASSETS
I'LL PUT IT INTO THE TECH STOCK
THEN BEFORE THE END OF THE MONTH
WE SELL, YOU RETURN THE PRINCIPLE,
AND WE RAKE IN THE CASH!
NO ONE WILL EVER NOTICE IT WAS EVEN GONE!
BESIDES, ISN'T IT REALLY YOUR INHERITANCE?
♩ YOUR CUPCAKE IS GETTING COLD ♫
COMMERCIAL ACCOUNT
AVAILABLE BAL
HELLOOOOOH
FIRST NATIONA
TAK TAK
TAKITY
FLIP
TAK TAK
FLP
JASE, C'MON...
God
WILL YOU JUST
shut up
AND LET ME FINISH THIS?
MM? WHADDSAY?
tak
LAMBDA DELT LAMBDA DELT HUH!
I JUST MADE FIFTEEN THOUSA DOLLARS
WELL...
GREAT...
NOW C'MERE, OKAY?

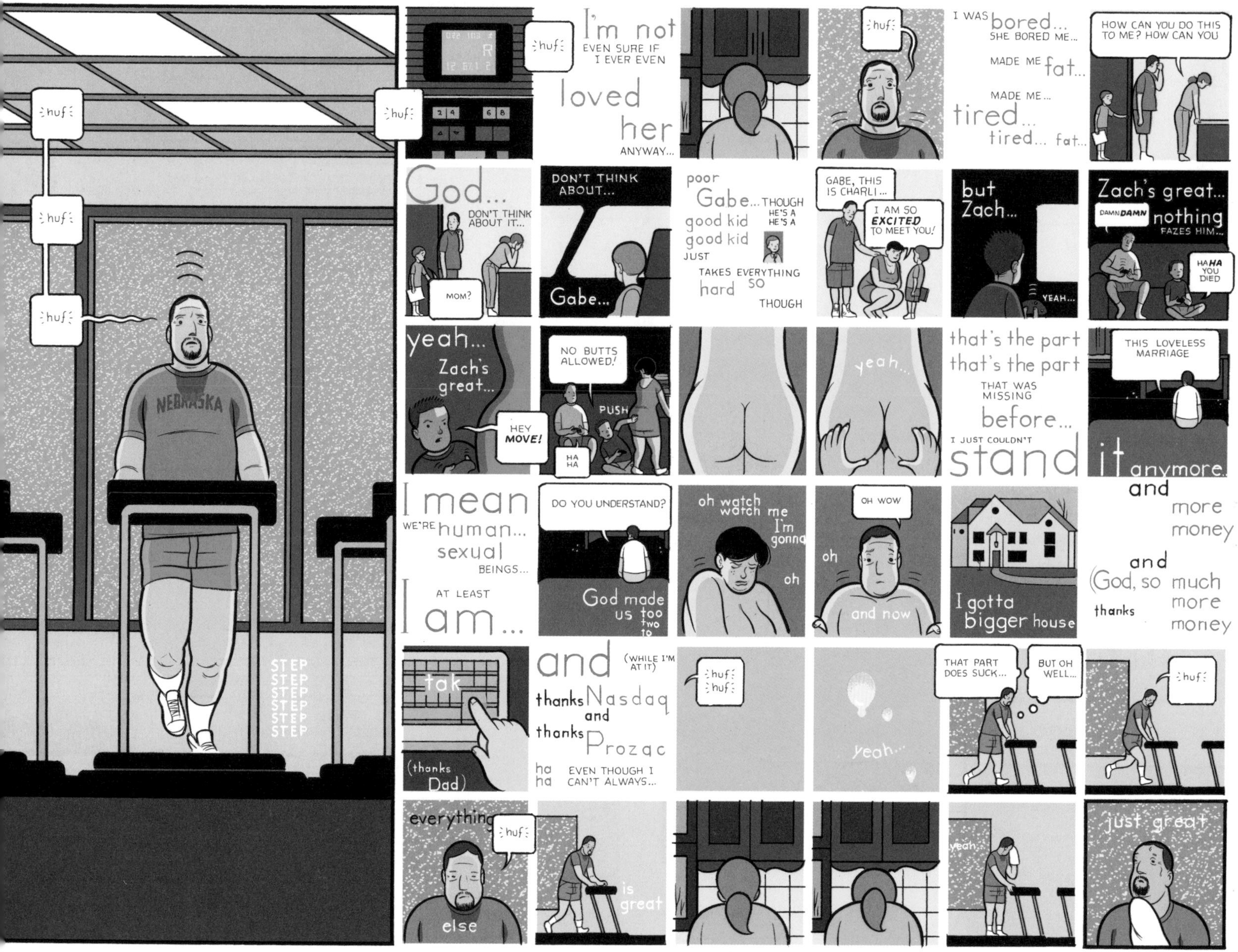
huf
huf
huf
huf
huf
STEP STEP STEP STEP STEP STEP
huf
I'm not EVEN SURE IF I EVER EVEN loved her ANYWAY...
huf
I WAS bored... SHE BORED ME...
MADE ME fat...
MADE ME... tired... tired... fat...
HOW CAN YOU DO THIS TO ME? HOW CAN YOU
God...
DON'T THINK ABOUT IT...
MOM?
DON'T THINK ABOUT...
Gabe...
poor Gabe... THOUGH HE'S A HE'S A good kid good kid
JUST TAKES EVERYTHING SO hard THOUGH
GABE, THIS IS CHARLI...
I AM SO EXCITED TO MEET YOU!
but Zach...
YEAH...
Zach's great...
DAMN DAMN
nothing FAZES HIM...
HA HA YOU DIED
yeah... Zach's great...
HEY MOVE!
NO BUTTS ALLOWED!
PUSH
HA HA
yeah...
that's the part that's the part THAT WAS MISSING before...
I JUST COULDN'T stand
THIS LOVELESS MARRIAGE
it anymore.
I mean WE'RE human... sexual BEINGS...
AT LEAST I am...
DO YOU UNDERSTAND?
God made us too two to
oh watch watch me I'm gonna
oh
OH WOW
oh
and now
I gotta bigger house
and more money
and (God, so much more money
thanks
tak
(thanks Dad)
and (WHILE I'M AT IT)
thanks Nasdaq and thanks Prozac
ha ha
EVEN THOUGH I CAN'T ALWAYS...
huf huf
yeah...
THAT PART DOES SUCK...
BUT OH WELL...
huf
everything
huf
else
is great
yeah
just great

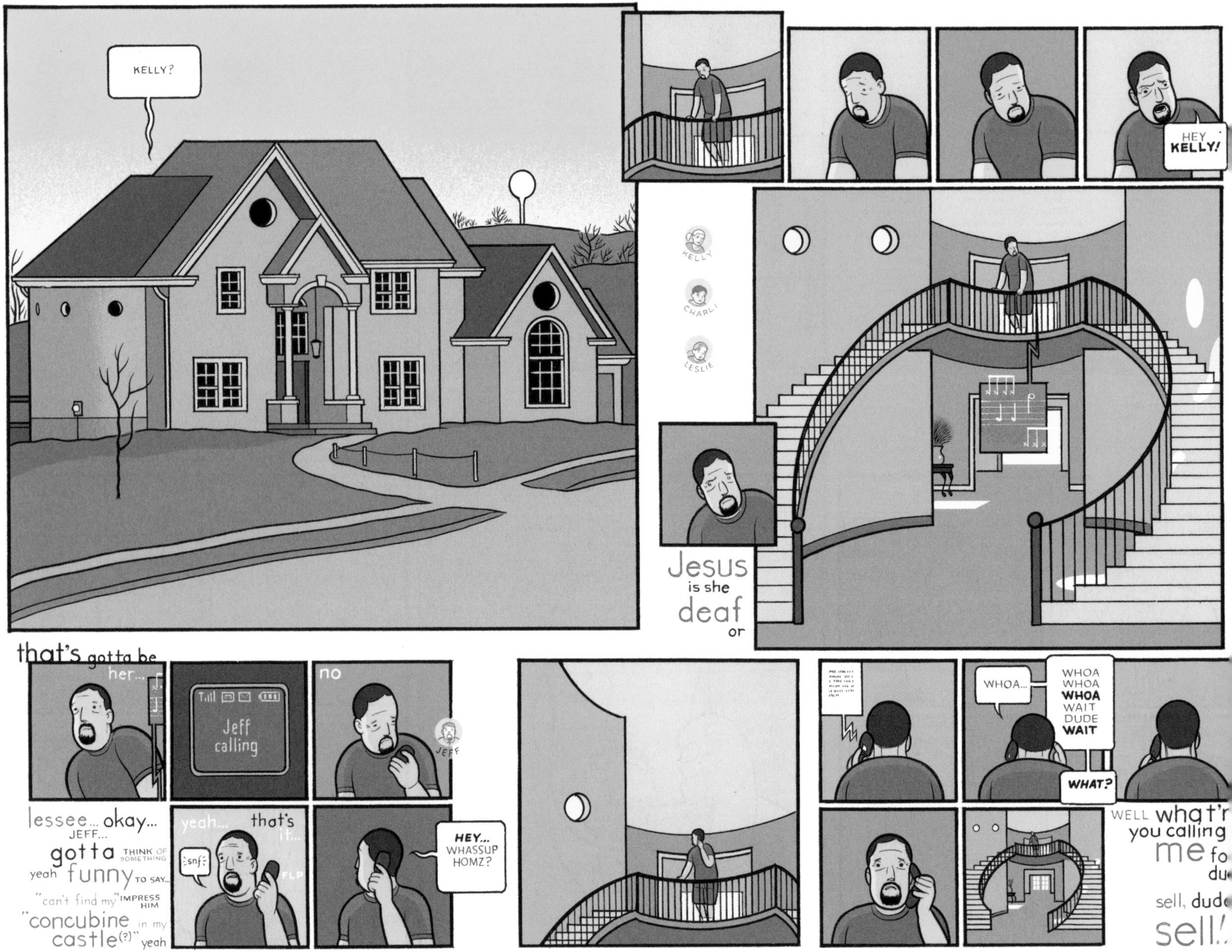
KELLY?
HEY KELLY!
KELLY
CHARLI
LESLIE
Jesus
is she
deaf
or
that's gotta be
her...
Jeff calling
no
JEFF
lessee... okay...
JEFF...
gotta THINK OF SOMETHING
yeah funny TO SAY...
"can't find my" IMPRESS HIM
"concubine in my
castle(?)" yeah
yeah...
that's it...
snf
FLP
HEY...
WHASSUP
HOMZ?
WHOA...
WHOA
WHOA
WHOA
WAIT
DUDE
WAIT
WHAT?
WELL what'r
you calling
me fo
du
sell, dude
sell!

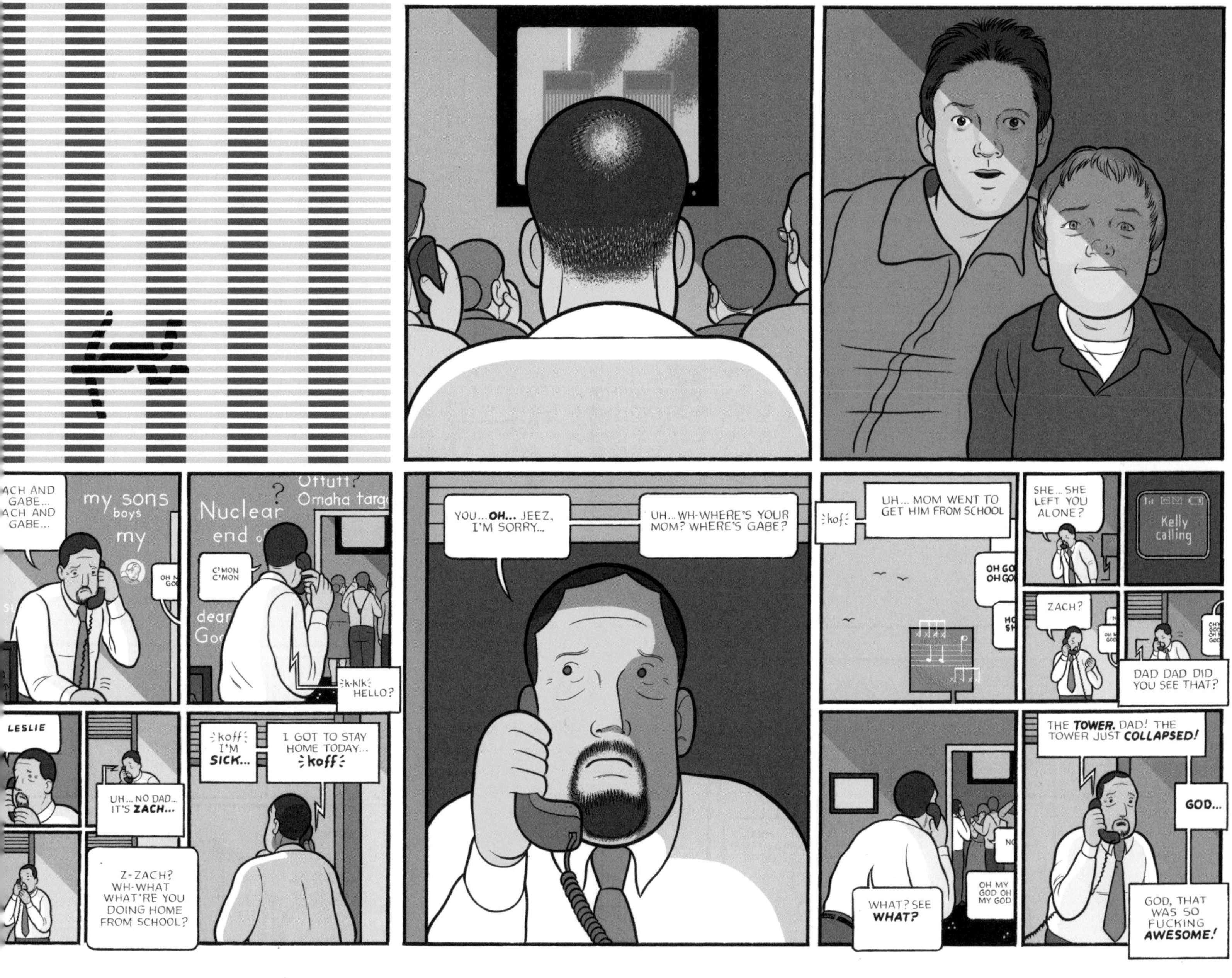

ACH AND GABE... ACH AND GABE...
my sons
boys
my
Nuclear
end of
?
Offutt?
Omaha targ
C'MON C'MON
dear
God
k-klk HELLO?
LESLIE
UH... NO DAD... IT'S ZACH...
Z-ZACH? WH-WHAT WHAT'RE YOU DOING HOME FROM SCHOOL?
koff I'M SICK...
I GOT TO STAY HOME TODAY... koff
YOU... OH... JEEZ, I'M SORRY...
UH... WH-WHERE'S YOUR MOM? WHERE'S GABE?
kof
UH... MOM WENT TO GET HIM FROM SCHOOL
SHE... SHE LEFT YOU ALONE?
Kelly calling
ZACH?
DAD DAD DID YOU SEE THAT?
WHAT? SEE WHAT?
OH MY GOD OH MY GOD
THE TOWER, DAD! THE TOWER JUST COLLAPSED!
GOD...
GOD, THAT WAS SO FUCKING AWESOME!

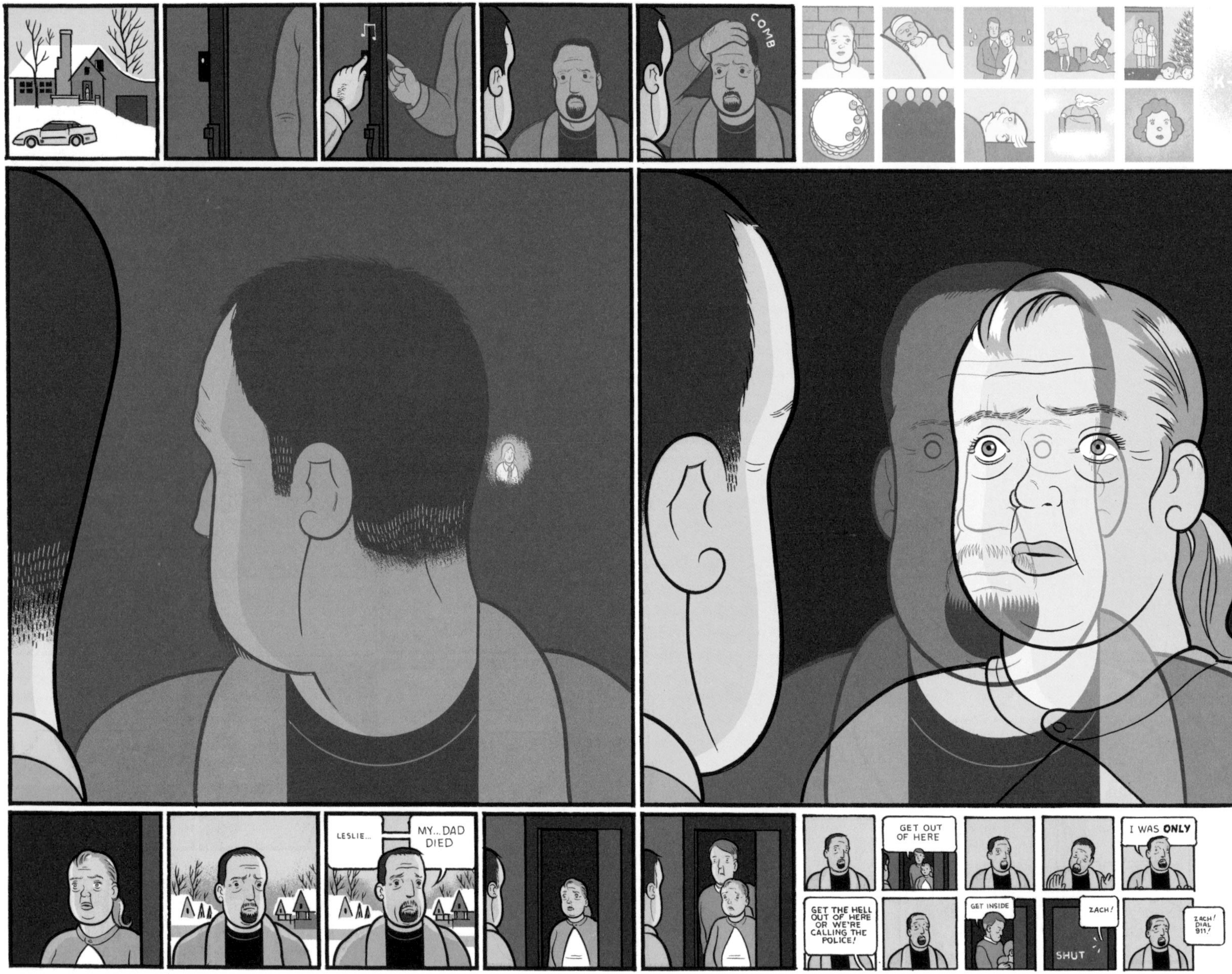

COMB
LESLIE...
MY... DAD DIED
GET OUT OF HERE
I WAS **ONLY**
GET THE HELL OUT OF HERE OR WE'RE CALLING THE POLICE!
GET INSIDE
ZACH!
SHUT
ZACH! DIAL 911!

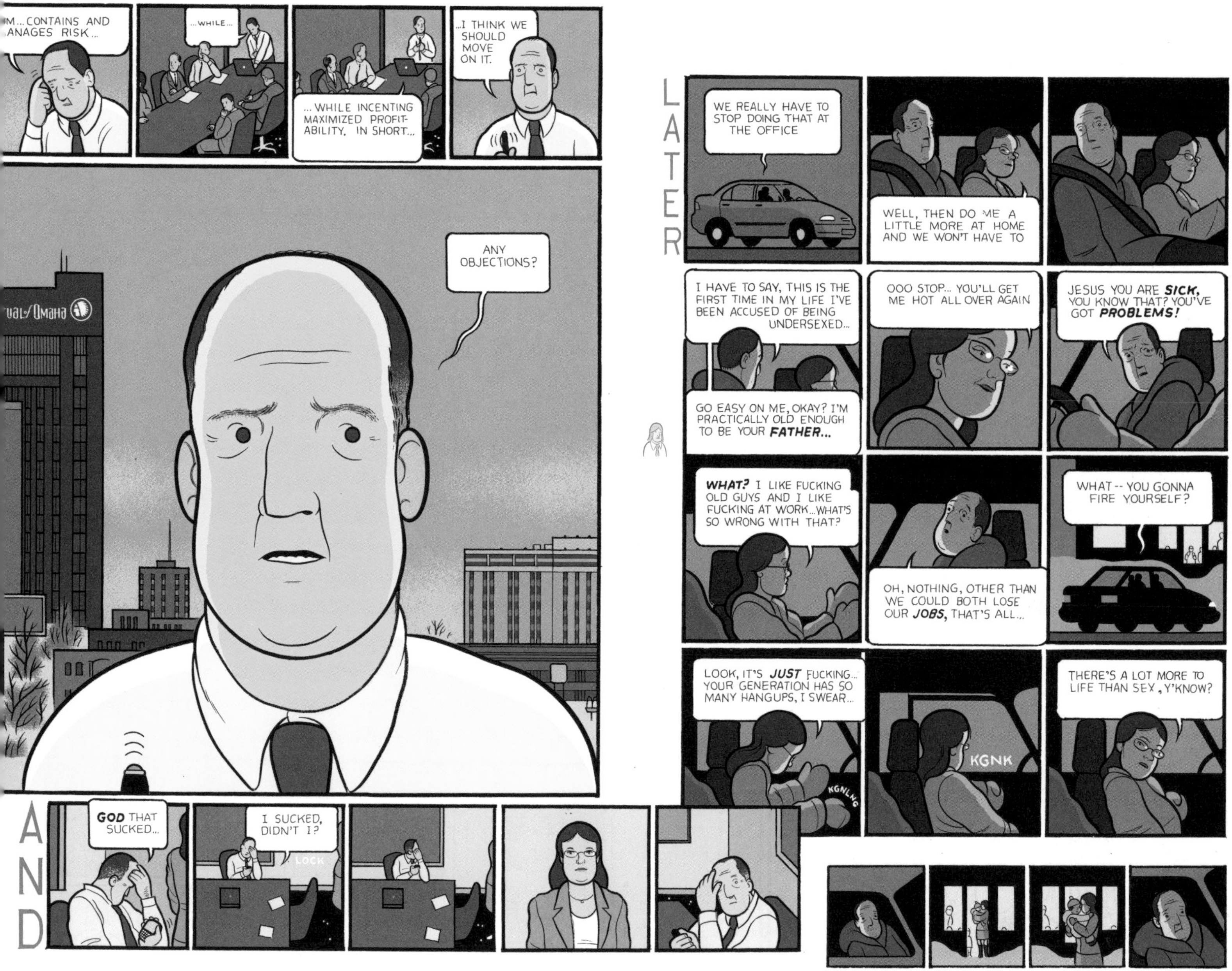

M... CONTAINS AND
ANAGES RISK...
...WHILE...
...WHILE INCENTING MAXIMIZED PROFIT-ABILITY. IN SHORT...
...I THINK WE SHOULD MOVE ON IT.
ANY OBJECTIONS?
AND
GOD THAT SUCKED...
I SUCKED, DIDN'T I?
LOCK
LATER
WE REALLY HAVE TO STOP DOING THAT AT THE OFFICE
WELL, THEN DO ME A LITTLE MORE AT HOME AND WE WON'T HAVE TO
I HAVE TO SAY, THIS IS THE FIRST TIME IN MY LIFE I'VE BEEN ACCUSED OF BEING UNDERSEXED...
GO EASY ON ME, OKAY? I'M PRACTICALLY OLD ENOUGH TO BE YOUR FATHER...
OOO STOP... YOU'LL GET ME HOT ALL OVER AGAIN
JESUS YOU ARE SICK, YOU KNOW THAT? YOU'VE GOT PROBLEMS!
WHAT? I LIKE FUCKING OLD GUYS AND I LIKE FUCKING AT WORK...WHAT'S SO WRONG WITH THAT?
OH, NOTHING, OTHER THAN WE COULD BOTH LOSE OUR JOBS, THAT'S ALL...
WHAT -- YOU GONNA FIRE YOURSELF?
LOOK, IT'S JUST FUCKING... YOUR GENERATION HAS SO MANY HANGUPS, I SWEAR...
KGNLNG
KGNK
THERE'S A LOT MORE TO LIFE THAN SEX, Y'KNOW?

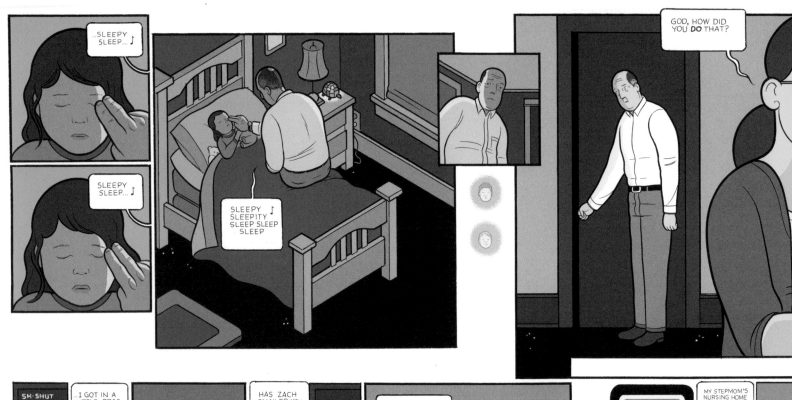

GOD, HOW DID YOU *DO* THAT?

...SLEEPY SLEEP... ♪

SLEEPY SLEEP... ♪

SLEEPY ♪ SLEEPITY SLEEP SLEEP SLEEP

SH-SHUT

OOH...

...I GOT IN A LITTLE PRACTICE WITH MY KIDS BEFORE MY LIFE FELL APART...

I'M SORRY

HAS ZACH EMAILED YOU BACK YET?

NAH

:koff:

POUR

EH...IT'S ALL MY FAULT

SET

I PROBABLY WON'T HEAR FROM HIM AGAIN UNTIL HE'S 18 AND NEEDS MONEY

JESUS, WHO'S CALLING ME AT--

SET

Happy Hollow House

MY STEPMOM'S NURSING HOME

THIS IS JO

I UNDERSTAND

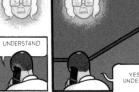

YES, I UNDERSTA

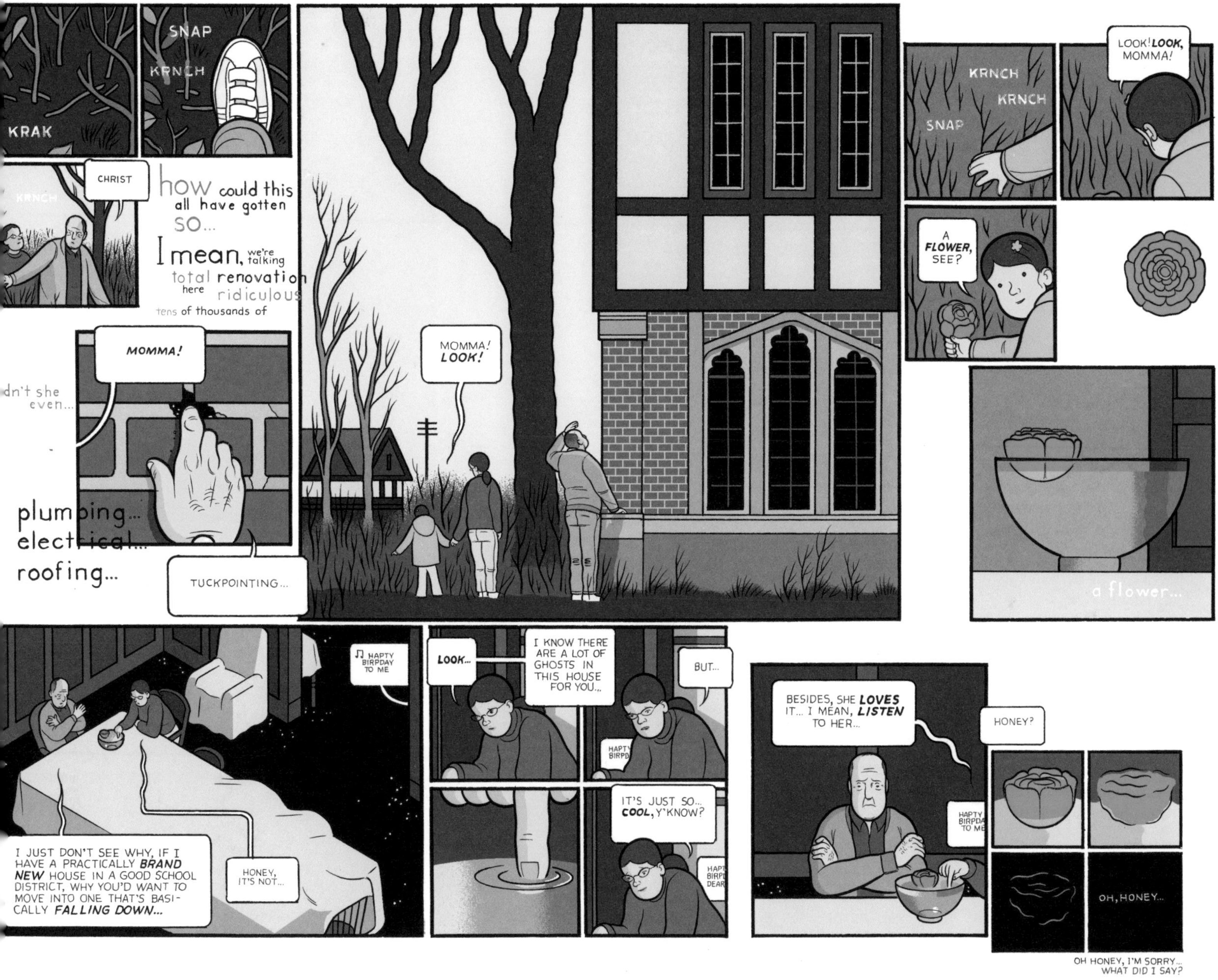
KRAK
SNAP
KRNCH
KRNCH
CHRIST
how could this all have gotten so...
I mean, we're talking total renovation here ridiculous
tens of thousands of
MOMMA!
dn't she even...
plumbing... electrical... roofing...
TUCKPOINTING...
MOMMA! LOOK!
KRNCH
KRNCH
SNAP
LOOK! LOOK, MOMMA!
A FLOWER, SEE?
a flower...
♫ HAPTY BIRPDAY TO ME
I JUST DON'T SEE WHY, IF I HAVE A PRACTICALLY BRAND NEW HOUSE IN A GOOD SCHOOL DISTRICT, WHY YOU'D WANT TO MOVE INTO ONE THAT'S BASICALLY FALLING DOWN...
HONEY, IT'S NOT...
LOOK...
I KNOW THERE ARE A LOT OF GHOSTS IN THIS HOUSE FOR YOU...
BUT...
IT'S JUST SO... COOL, Y'KNOW?
BESIDES, SHE LOVES IT... I MEAN, LISTEN TO HER...
HAPTY BIRPDA TO ME
HONEY?
OH, HONEY...
OH HONEY, I'M SORRY... WHAT DID I SAY?

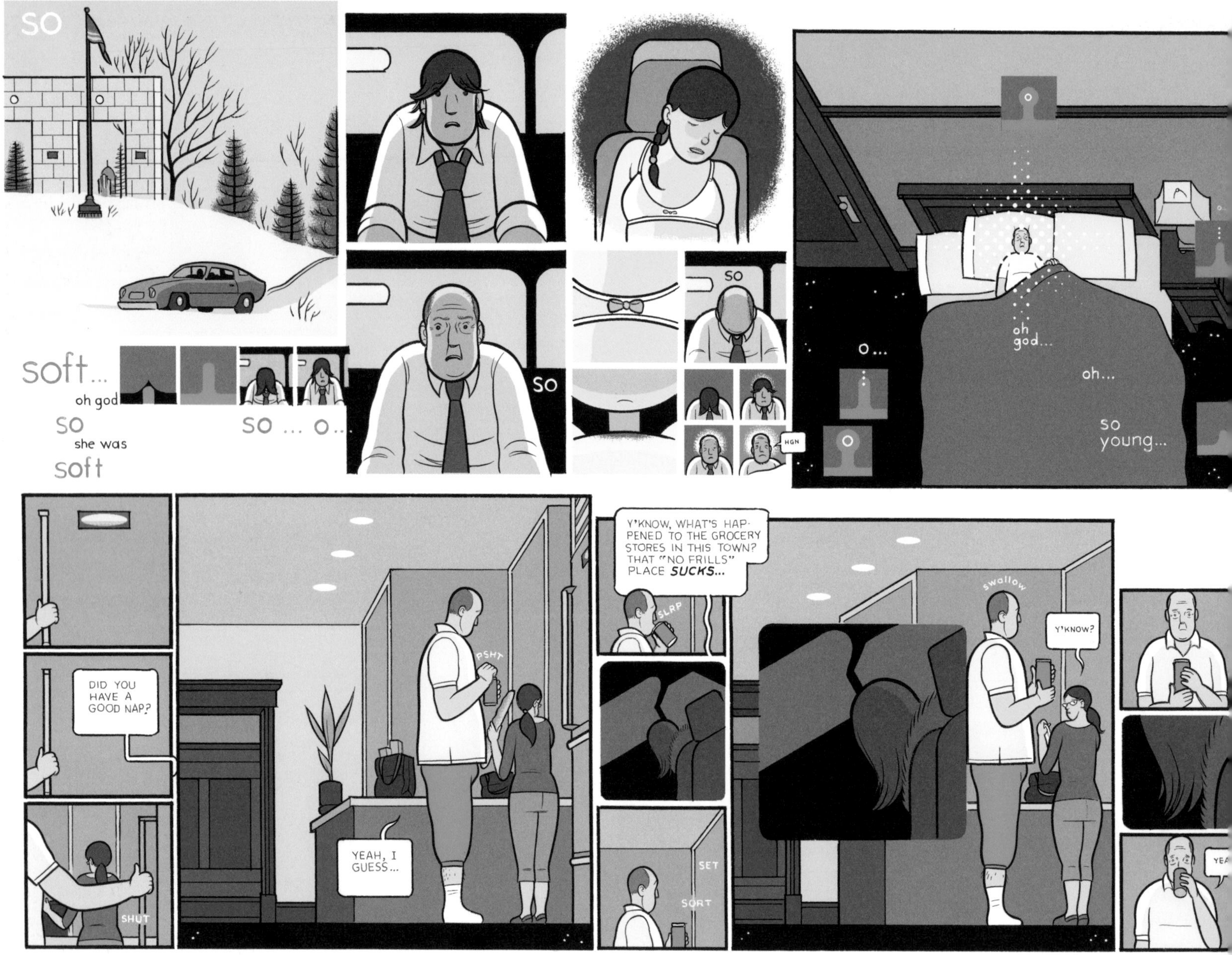
SO
soft...
oh god
so
she was
soft
SO ... O...
SO
SO
HGN
O...
oh
god...
oh...
so
young...
DID YOU HAVE A GOOD NAP?
SHUT
PSHT
YEAH, I GUESS...
Y'KNOW, WHAT'S HAP-PENED TO THE GROCERY STORES IN THIS TOWN? THAT "NO FRILLS" PLACE **SUCKS...**
SLRP
SET
SORT
swallow
Y'KNOW?

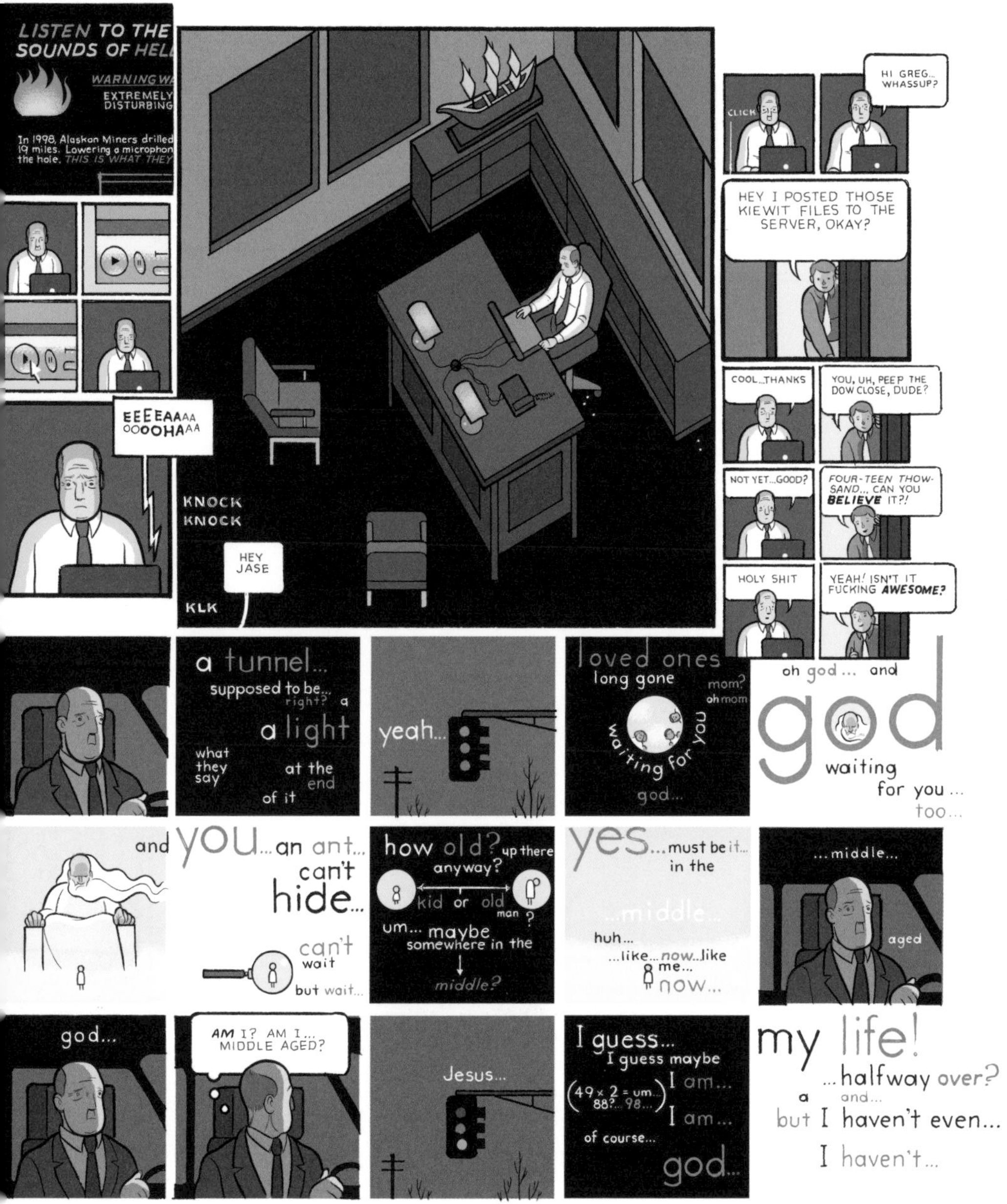
LISTEN TO THE
SOUNDS OF HEL
WARNING WA
EXTREMELY DISTURBING
In 1998, Alaskan Miners drilled
19 miles. Lowering a microphon
the hole. THIS IS WHAT THEY
EEEEAAAA OOOOHAAA
KNOCK KNOCK
HEY JASE
KLK
CLICK
HI GREG... WHASSUP?
HEY I POSTED THOSE KIEWIT FILES TO THE SERVER, OKAY?
COOL...THANKS
YOU, UH, PEEP THE DOW CLOSE, DUDE?
NOT YET...GOOD?
FOUR-TEEN THOW-SAND... CAN YOU BELIEVE IT?!
HOLY SHIT
YEAH! ISN'T IT FUCKING AWESOME?
a tunnel... supposed to be... right? a light what they say at the end of it
yeah...
loved ones long gone mom? oh mom waiting for you god...
oh god... and god waiting for you... too...
and you... an ant... can't hide... can't wait but wait...
how old? up there anyway? kid or old man? um... maybe somewhere in the middle?
yes... must be it... in the ...middle... huh... like... now... like me... now...
...middle... aged
god...
AM I? AM I... MIDDLE AGED?
Jesus...
I guess... I guess maybe I am... I am... (49 x 2 = um... 88?... 98...) of course... god...
my life! ...halfway over? a and... but I haven't even... I haven't...

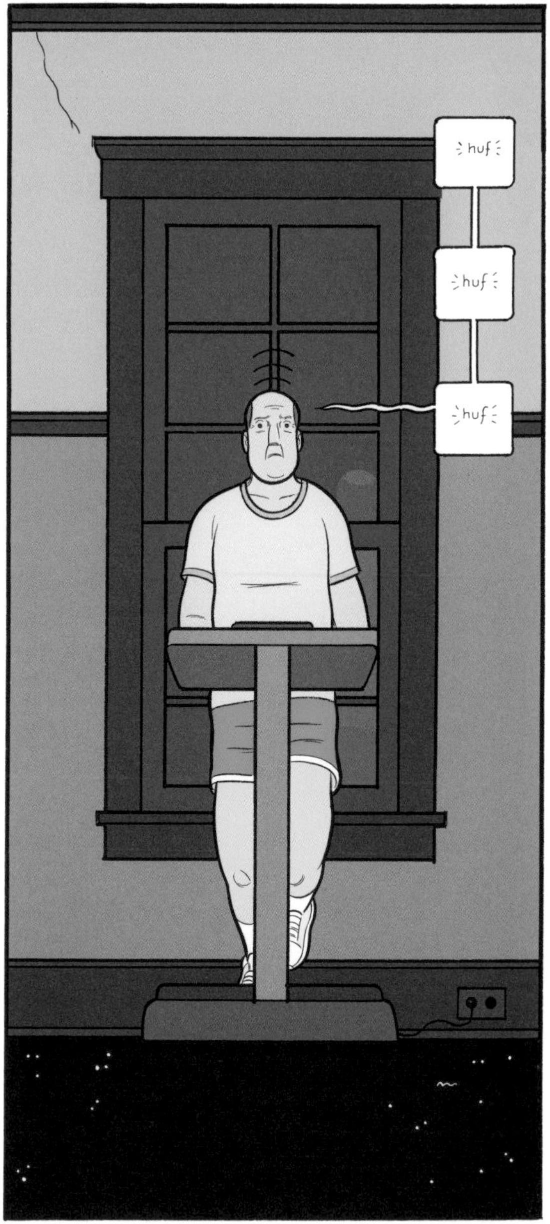
huf
huf
huf

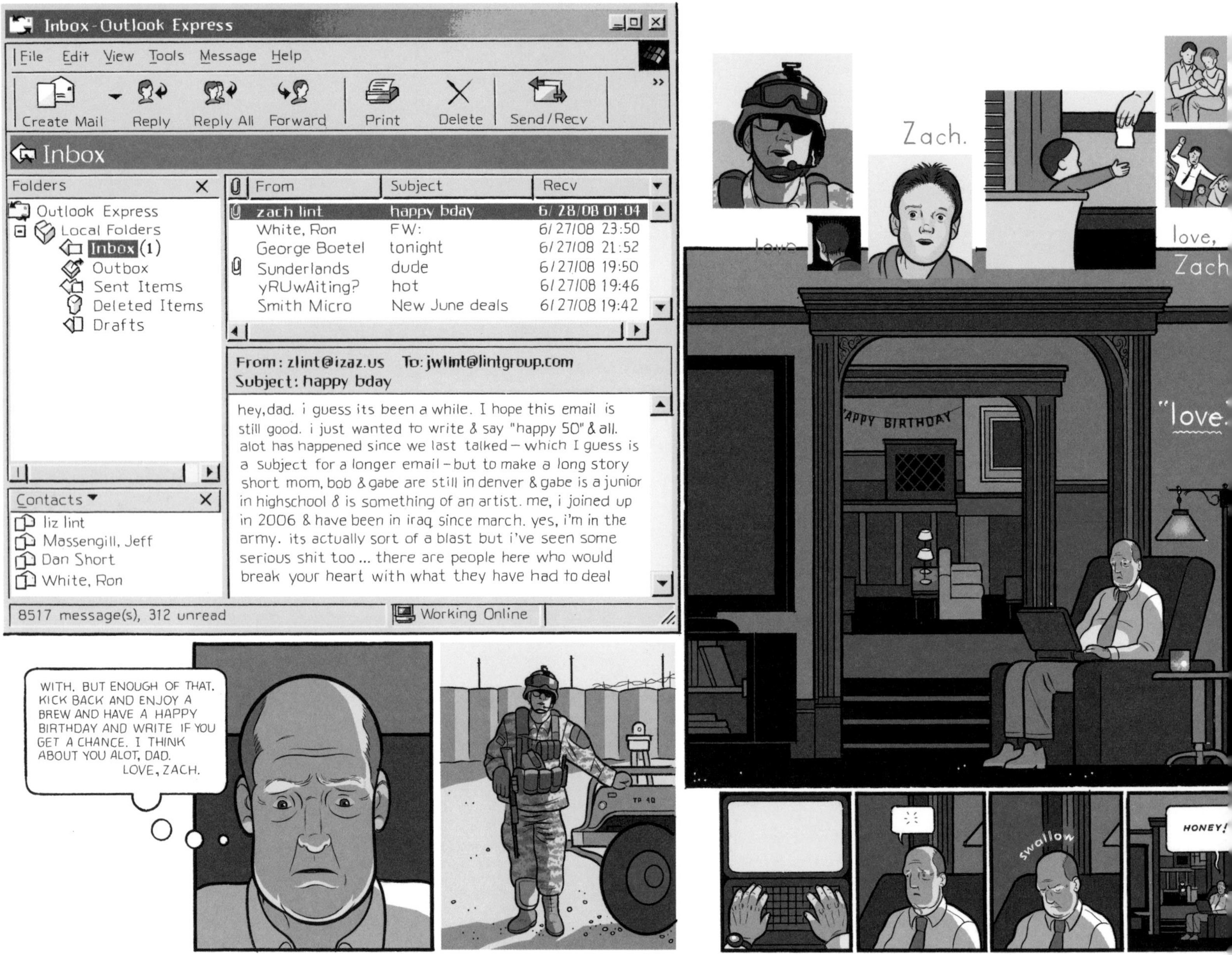

Inbox - Outlook Express
File Edit View Tools Message Help
Create Mail Reply Reply All Forward Print Delete Send/Recv
Inbox
Folders
Outlook Express
Local Folders
Inbox (1)
Outbox
Sent Items
Deleted Items
Drafts
From Subject Recv
zach lint happy bday 6/28/08 01:04
White, Ron FW: 6/27/08 23:50
George Boetel tonight 6/27/08 21:52
Sunderlands dude 6/27/08 19:50
yRUwAiting? hot 6/27/08 19:46
Smith Micro New June deals 6/27/08 19:42
From: zlint@izaz.us To: jwlint@lintgroup.com
Subject: happy bday
hey, dad. i guess its been a while. I hope this email is still good. i just wanted to write & say "happy 50" & all. alot has happened since we last talked – which I guess is a subject for a longer email – but to make a long story short mom, bob & gabe are still in denver & gabe is a junior in highschool & is something of an artist. me, i joined up in 2006 & have been in iraq since march. yes, i'm in the army. its actually sort of a blast but i've seen some serious shit too ... there are people here who would break your heart with what they have had to deal
Contacts
liz lint
Massengill, Jeff
Dan Short
White, Ron
8517 message(s), 312 unread
Working Online
WITH. BUT ENOUGH OF THAT. KICK BACK AND ENJOY A BREW AND HAVE A HAPPY BIRTHDAY AND WRITE IF YOU GET A CHANCE. I THINK ABOUT YOU ALOT, DAD. LOVE, ZACH.
TP 40
Zach.
love
love,
Zach
"love."
HAPPY BIRTHDAY
swallow
HONEY!

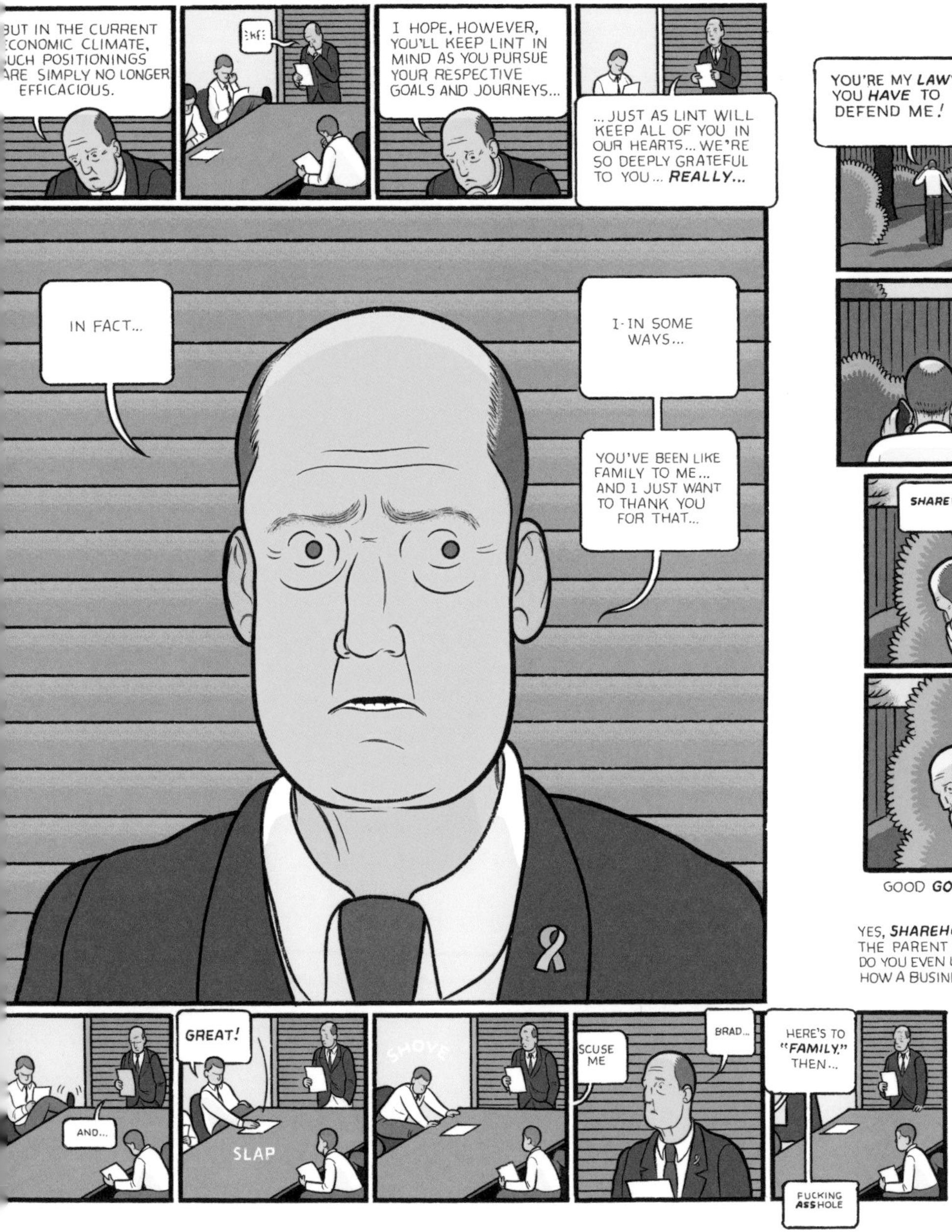

BUT IN THE CURRENT ECONOMIC CLIMATE, SUCH POSITIONINGS ARE SIMPLY NO LONGER EFFICACIOUS.
I HOPE, HOWEVER, YOU'LL KEEP LINT IN MIND AS YOU PURSUE YOUR RESPECTIVE GOALS AND JOURNEYS...
... JUST AS LINT WILL KEEP ALL OF YOU IN OUR HEARTS... WE'RE SO DEEPLY GRATEFUL TO YOU... REALLY...
IN FACT...
I-IN SOME WAYS...
YOU'VE BEEN LIKE FAMILY TO ME... AND I JUST WANT TO THANK YOU FOR THAT...
AND...
GREAT!
SLAP
SHOVE
SCUSE ME
BRAD...
HERE'S TO "FAMILY," THEN...
FUCKING ASSHOLE

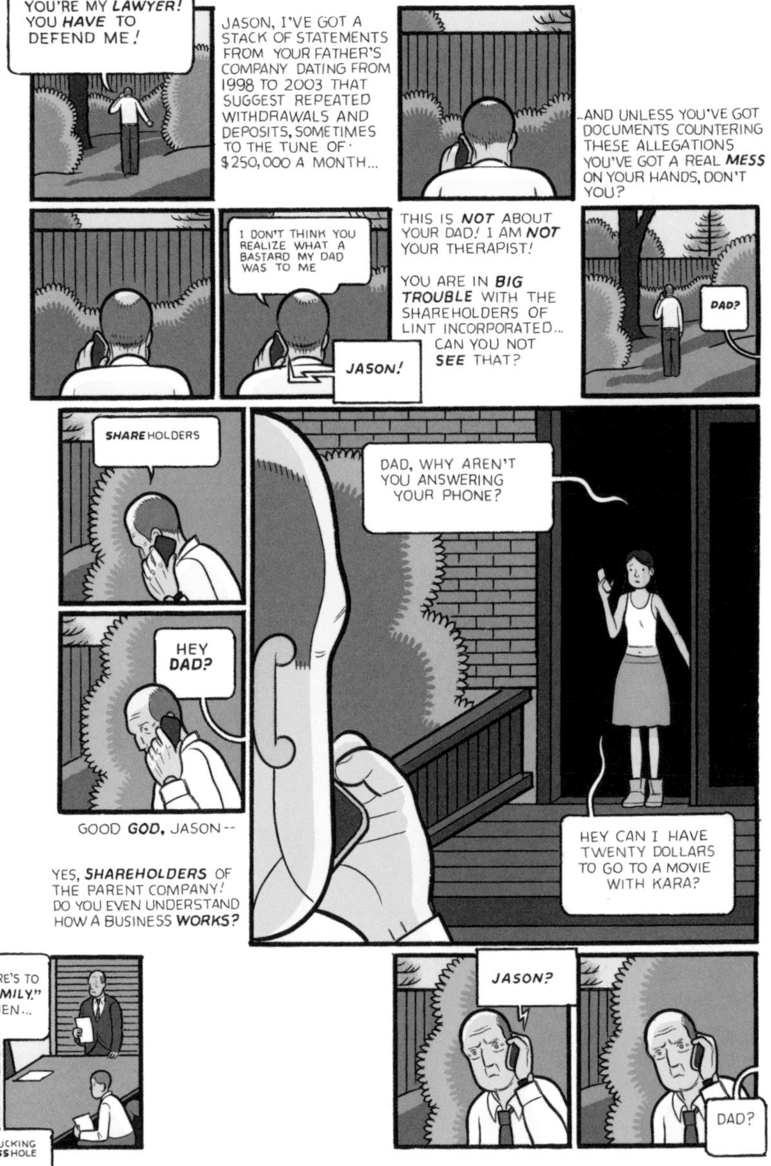

YOU'RE MY LAWYER! YOU HAVE TO DEFEND ME!
JASON, I'VE GOT A STACK OF STATEMENTS FROM YOUR FATHER'S COMPANY DATING FROM 1998 TO 2003 THAT SUGGEST REPEATED WITHDRAWALS AND DEPOSITS, SOMETIMES TO THE TUNE OF $250,000 A MONTH...
...AND UNLESS YOU'VE GOT DOCUMENTS COUNTERING THESE ALLEGATIONS YOU'VE GOT A REAL MESS ON YOUR HANDS, DON'T YOU?
I DON'T THINK YOU REALIZE WHAT A BASTARD MY DAD WAS TO ME
JASON!
THIS IS NOT ABOUT YOUR DAD! I AM NOT YOUR THERAPIST!
YOU ARE IN BIG TROUBLE WITH THE SHAREHOLDERS OF LINT INCORPORATED... CAN YOU NOT SEE THAT?
DAD?
SHAREHOLDERS
HEY DAD?
GOOD GOD, JASON--
YES, SHAREHOLDERS OF THE PARENT COMPANY! DO YOU EVEN UNDERSTAND HOW A BUSINESS WORKS?
DAD, WHY AREN'T YOU ANSWERING YOUR PHONE?
HEY CAN I HAVE TWENTY DOLLARS TO GO TO A MOVIE WITH KARA?
JASON?
DAD?

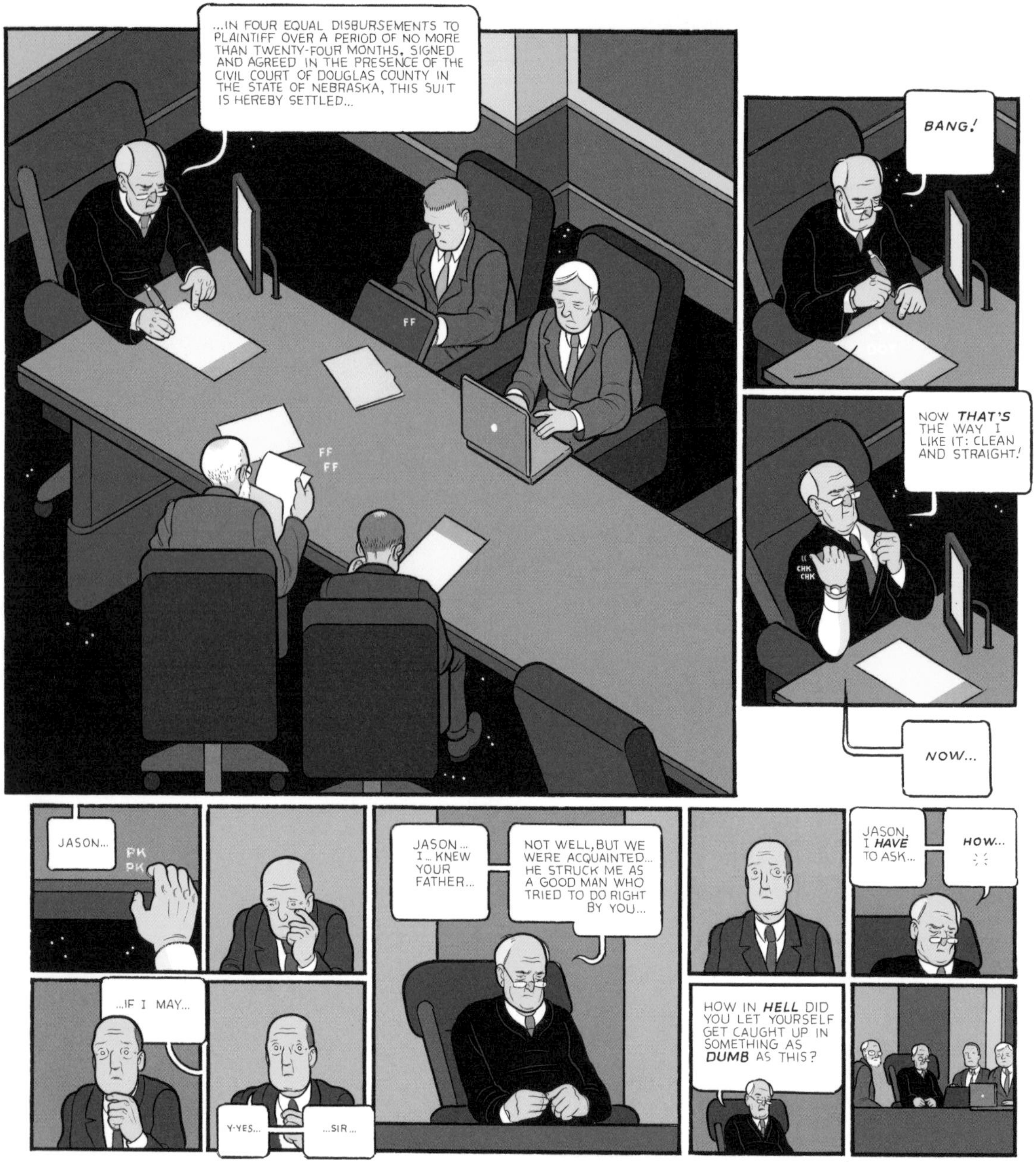
...IN FOUR EQUAL DISBURSEMENTS TO PLAINTIFF OVER A PERIOD OF NO MORE THAN TWENTY-FOUR MONTHS. SIGNED AND AGREED IN THE PRESENCE OF THE CIVIL COURT OF DOUGLAS COUNTY IN THE STATE OF NEBRASKA, THIS SUIT IS HEREBY SETTLED...
FF
FF
FF
BANG!
NOW THAT'S THE WAY I LIKE IT: CLEAN AND STRAIGHT!
CHK
CHK
NOW...
JASON...
PK
PK
...IF I MAY...
Y-YES...
...SIR...
JASON... I... KNEW YOUR FATHER...
NOT WELL, BUT WE WERE ACQUAINTED... HE STRUCK ME AS A GOOD MAN WHO TRIED TO DO RIGHT BY YOU...
JASON, I HAVE TO ASK...
HOW...
HOW IN HELL DID YOU LET YOURSELF GET CAUGHT UP IN SOMETHING AS DUMB AS THIS?

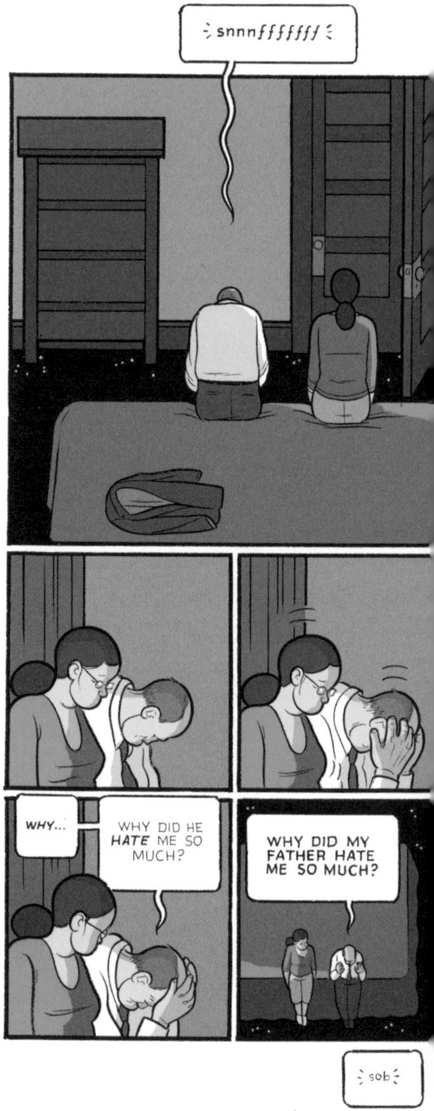
snnnfffffff
WHY...
WHY DID HE HATE ME SO MUCH?
WHY DID MY FATHER HATE ME SO MUCH?
sob

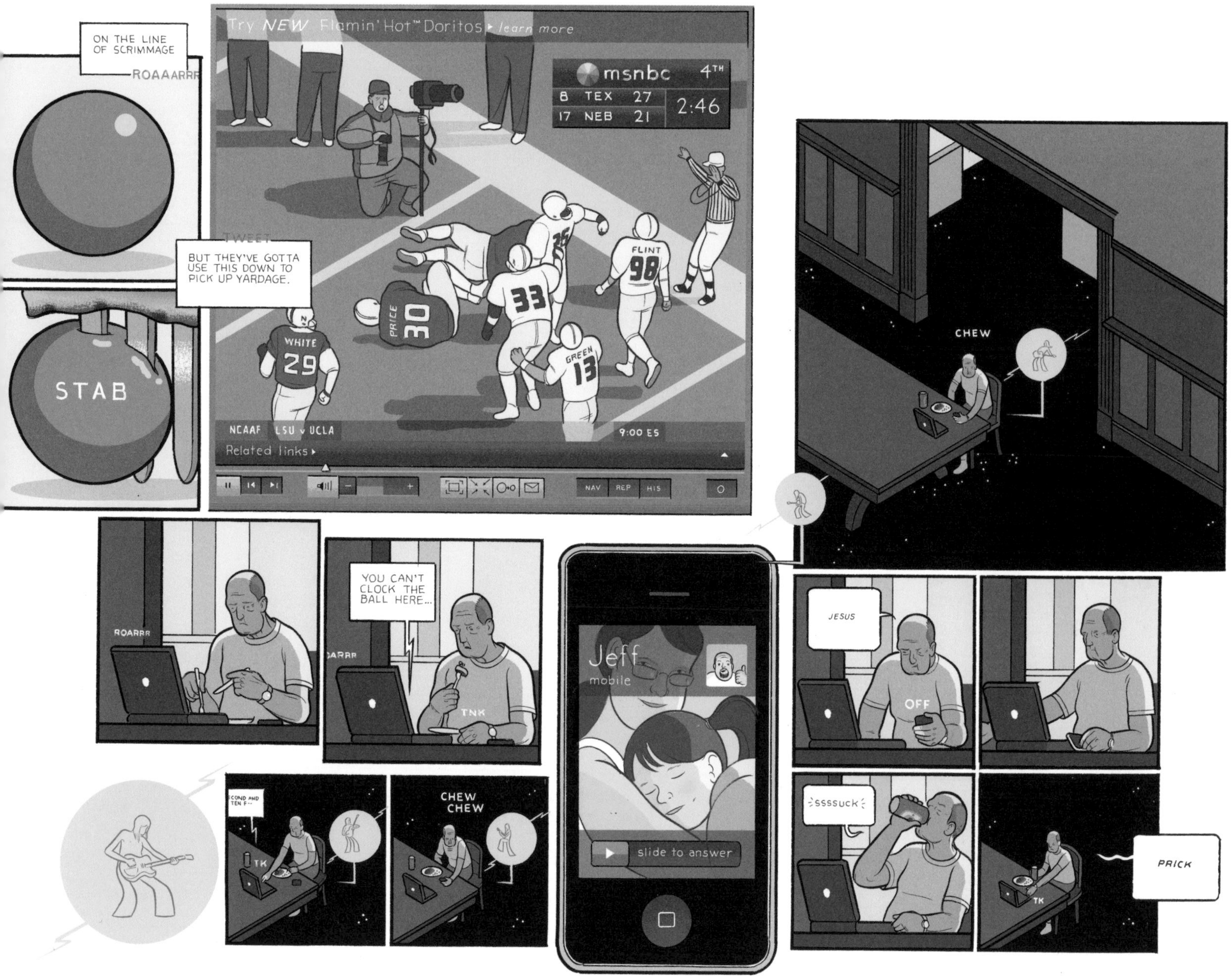

ON THE LINE OF SCRIMMAGE
ROAAARRR
STAB
Try NEW Flamin' Hot™ Doritos ▸ learn more
msnbc 4TH
8 TEX 27
17 NEB 21
2:46
BUT THEY'VE GOTTA USE THIS DOWN TO PICK UP YARDAGE.
FLINT 98
33
PRICE 30
WHITE 29
GREEN 13
NCAAF LSU v UCLA
9:00 ES
Related links ▸
NAV REP HIS
CHEW
ROARRR
YOU CAN'T CLOCK THE BALL HERE...
ARRR
TNK
Jeff
mobile
slide to answer
JESUS
OFF
TK
CHEW CHEW
SSSSUCK
PRICK
TK

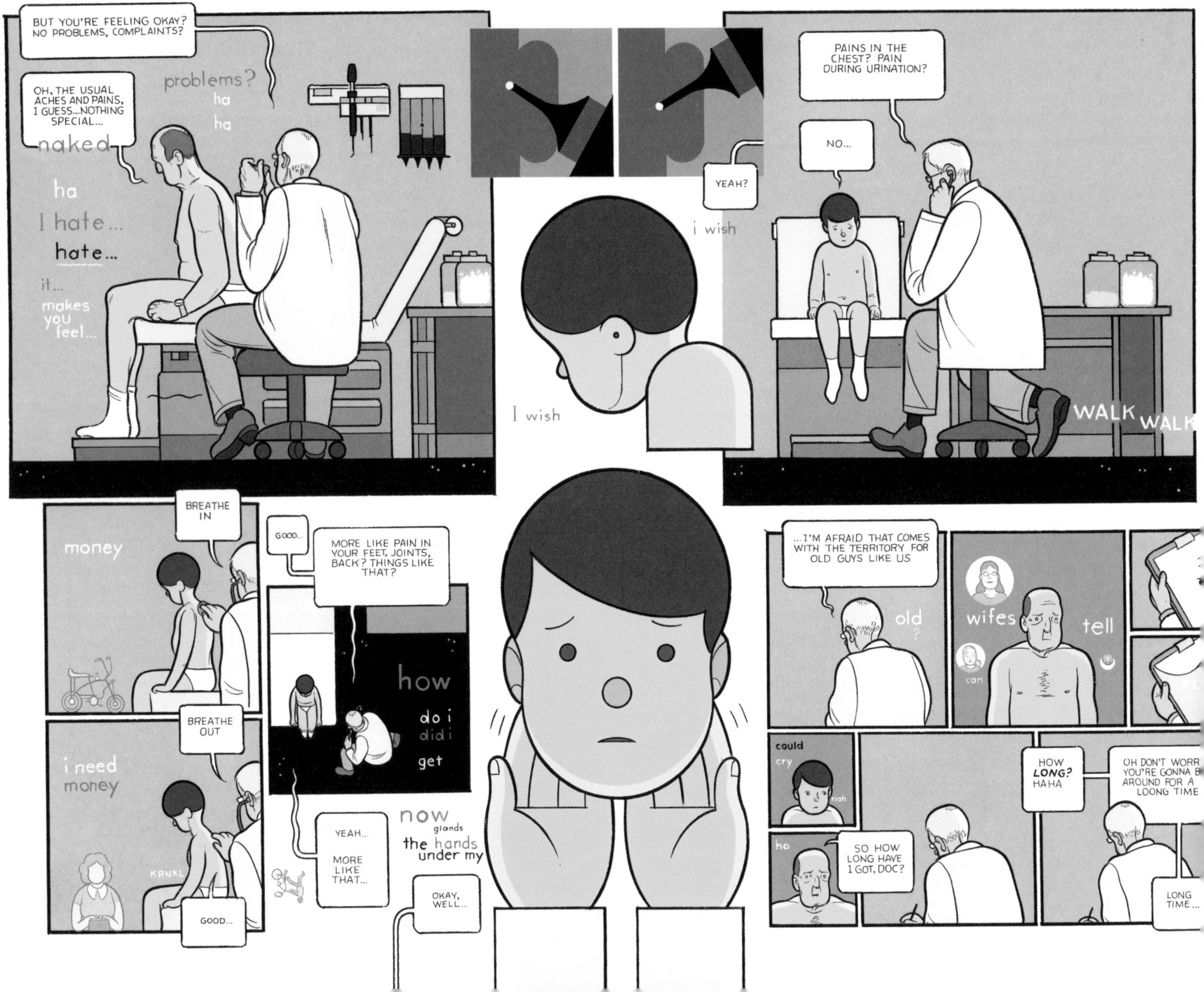

BUT YOU'RE FEELING OKAY? NO PROBLEMS, COMPLAINTS?
OH, THE USUAL ACHES AND PAINS, I GUESS...NOTHING SPECIAL...
problems?
ha
ha
naked
ha
I hate...
hate...
it...
makes you feel...
YEAH?
i wish
I wish
PAINS IN THE CHEST? PAIN DURING URINATION?
NO...
WALK
WALK
BREATHE IN
money
BREATHE OUT
i need money
KRNKL
GOOD...
GOOD...
MORE LIKE PAIN IN YOUR FEET, JOINTS, BACK? THINGS LIKE THAT?
how
do i
did i
get
YEAH...
MORE LIKE THAT...
now
glands
the hands
under my
OKAY, WELL...
...I'M AFRAID THAT COMES WITH THE TERRITORY FOR OLD GUYS LIKE US
old
?
wifes
tell
can
could
cry
nah
ha
SO HOW LONG HAVE I GOT, DOC?
HOW **LONG?** HAHA
LONG TIME...

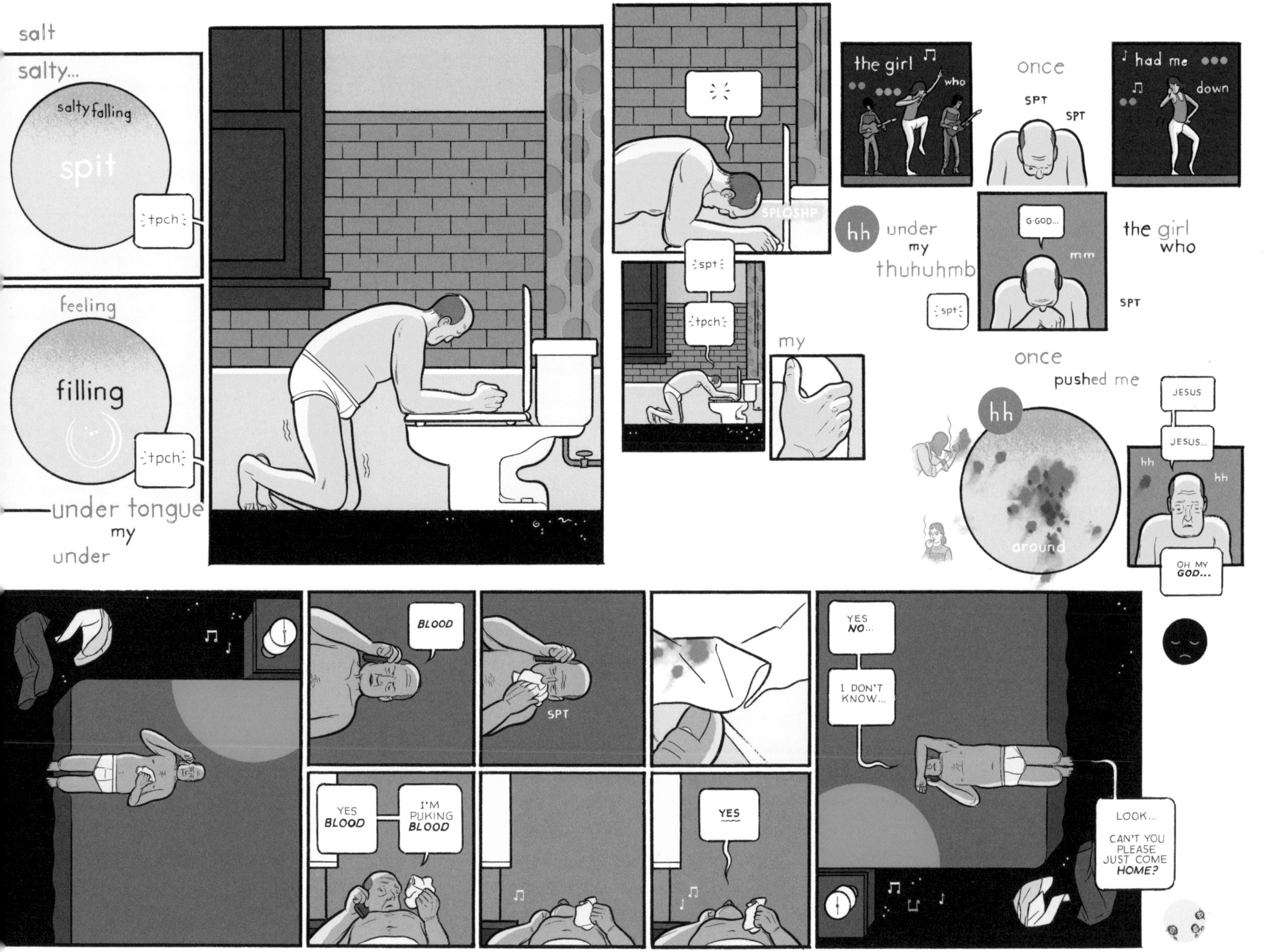

salt
salty...
salty falling
spit
tpch
feeling
filling
tpch
under tongue
my
under
SPLOSHP
spt
tpch
my
the girl
who
once
SPT
SPT
had me
down
hh
under
my
thuhuhmb
spt
G-GOD...
mm
SPT
the girl
who
once
pushed me
hh
around
JESUS
JESUS...
hh
hh
OH MY GOD...
BLOOD
SPT
YES BLOOD
I'M PUKING BLOOD
YES
YES NO...
I DON'T KNOW...
LOOK...
CAN'T YOU PLEASE JUST COME HOME?

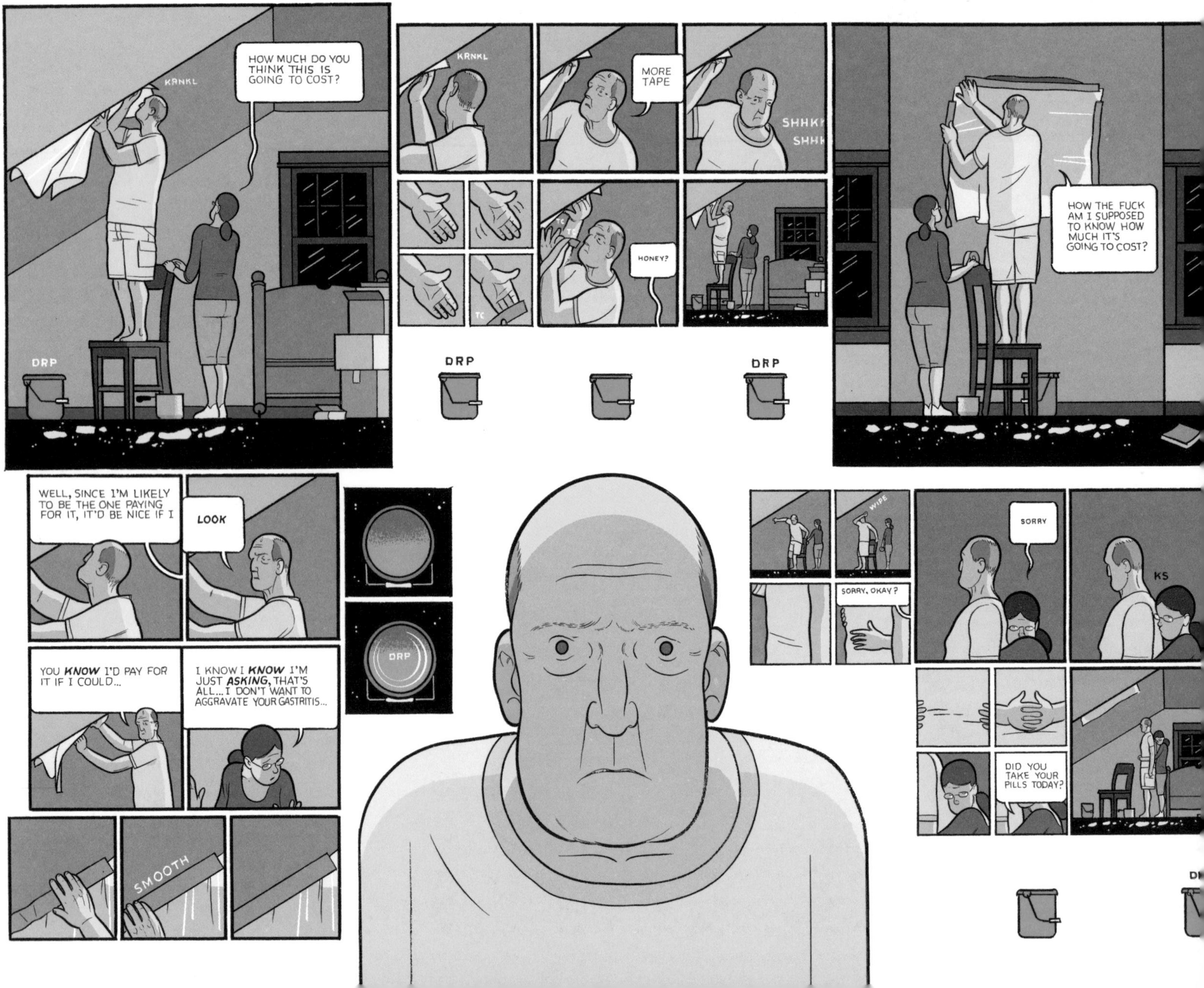

KRNKL
HOW MUCH DO YOU THINK THIS IS GOING TO COST?
DRP
KRNKL
MORE TAPE
SHHKK SHHK
TC
TC
TC
TC
HONEY?
DRP
DRP
HOW THE FUCK AM I SUPPOSED TO KNOW HOW MUCH IT'S GOING TO COST?
WELL, SINCE I'M LIKELY TO BE THE ONE PAYING FOR IT, IT'D BE NICE IF I
LOOK
YOU KNOW I'D PAY FOR IT IF I COULD...
I KNOW I KNOW I'M JUST ASKING, THAT'S ALL... I DON'T WANT TO AGGRAVATE YOUR GASTRITIS...
DRP
SMOOTH
WIPE
SORRY, OKAY?
SORRY
KS
DID YOU TAKE YOUR PILLS TODAY?

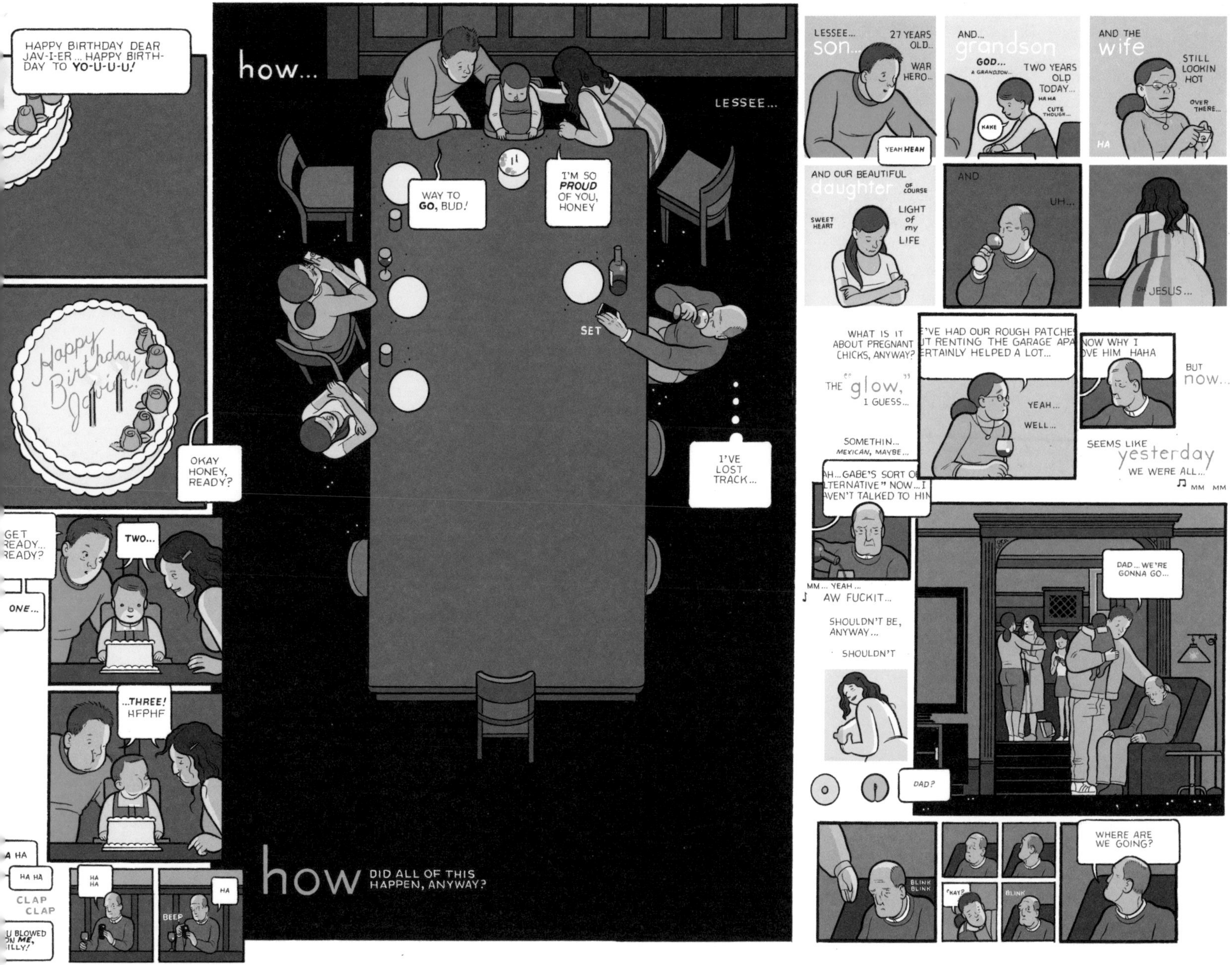

HAPPY BIRTHDAY DEAR JAV-I-ER... HAPPY BIRTH-DAY TO YO-U-U-U!
Happy Birthday Javier!
OKAY HONEY, READY?
GET
EADY...
EADY?
ONE...
TWO...
...THREE! HFPHF
A HA
HA HA
CLAP CLAP
U BLOWED ON ME, ILLY!
HA HA
BEEP
HA
how...
WAY TO GO, BUD!
I'M SO PROUD OF YOU, HONEY
LESSEE...
SET
I'VE LOST TRACK...
how DID ALL OF THIS HAPPEN, ANYWAY?
LESSEE... son...
27 YEARS OLD... WAR HERO...
YEAH HEAH
AND... grandson
GOD... A GRANDSON...
TWO YEARS OLD TODAY...
HA HA
CUTE THOUGH...
KAKE
AND THE wife
STILL LOOKIN HOT
OVER THERE...
HA
AND OUR BEAUTIFUL daughter
OF COURSE
SWEET HEART
LIGHT of my LIFE
AND
UH...
OH JESUS...
WHAT IS IT ABOUT PREGNANT CHICKS, ANYWAY?
THE "glow," I GUESS...
SOMETHIN... MEXICAN, MAYBE...
'VE HAD OUR ROUGH PATCHES
T RENTING THE GARAGE APA
ERTAINLY HELPED A LOT...
YEAH...
WELL...
NOW WHY I
OVE HIM HAHA
BUT now...
SEEMS LIKE yesterday WE WERE ALL...
MM MM
H... GABE'S SORT O
LTERNATIVE" NOW... I
AVEN'T TALKED TO HI
MM... YEAH...
AW FUCKIT...
SHOULDN'T BE, ANYWAY...
SHOULDN'T
DAD... WE'RE GONNA GO...
DAD?
BLINK BLINK
'KAY?
BLINK
WHERE ARE WE GOING?

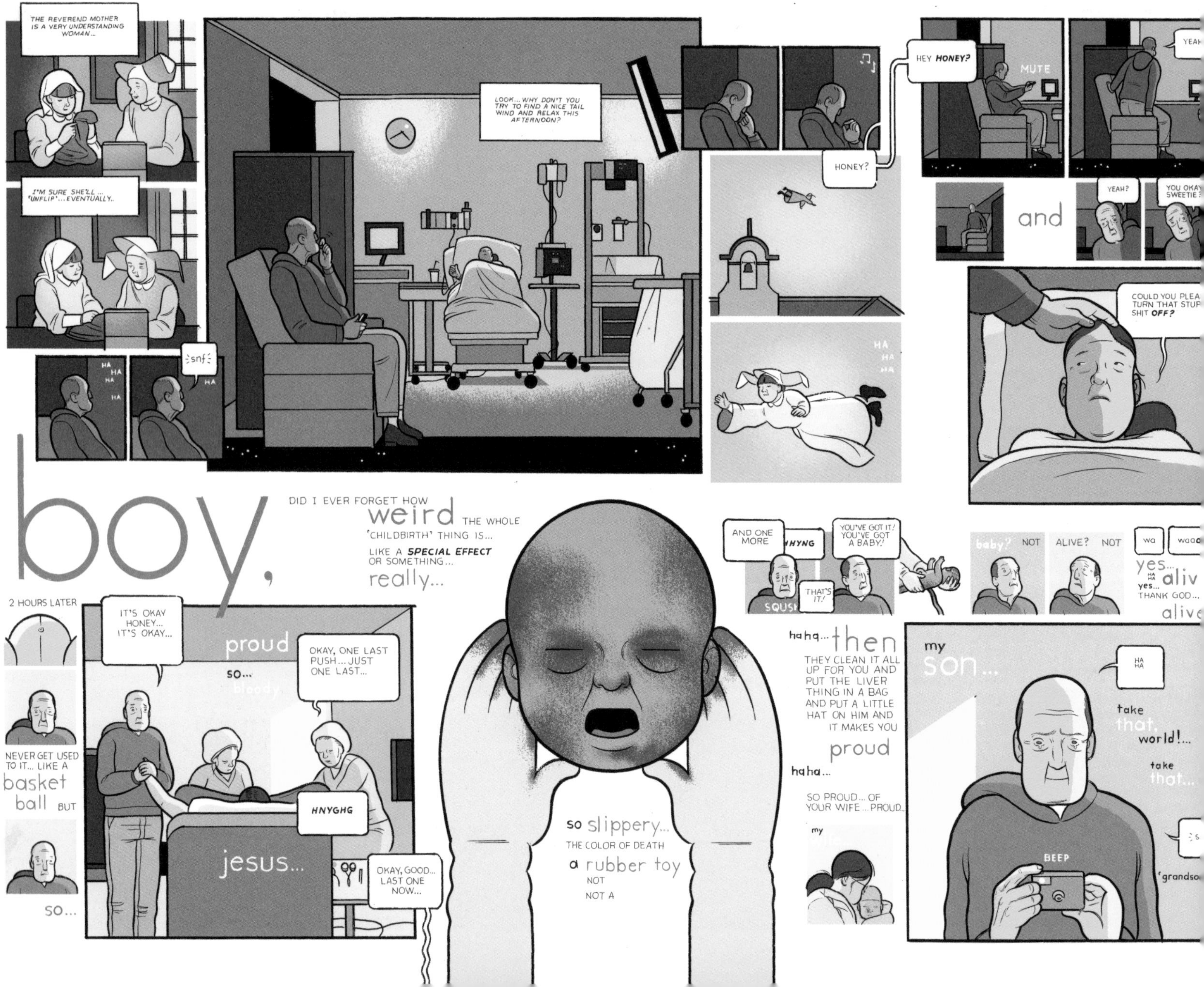

THE REVEREND MOTHER IS A VERY UNDERSTANDING WOMAN...
I'M SURE SHE'LL ... 'UNFLIP' ... EVENTUALLY..
HA HA HA HA
snf
HA
LOOK... WHY DON'T YOU TRY TO FIND A NICE TAIL WIND AND RELAX THIS AFTERNOON?
HEY HONEY?
HONEY?
HA HA HA
MUTE
YEAH
and
YEAH?
YOU OKAY SWEETIE?
COULD YOU PLEA TURN THAT STUP SHIT OFF?
boy,
DID I EVER FORGET HOW weird THE WHOLE 'CHILDBIRTH' THING IS...
LIKE A SPECIAL EFFECT OR SOMETHING...
really...
2 HOURS LATER
NEVER GET USED TO IT... LIKE A basket ball BUT
so...
IT'S OKAY HONEY... IT'S OKAY...
proud
SO...
bloody
OKAY, ONE LAST PUSH... JUST ONE LAST...
HNYGHG
jesus...
OKAY, GOOD... LAST ONE NOW...
so slippery...
THE COLOR OF DEATH
a rubber toy
NOT
NOT A
AND ONE MORE
HHYNG
SQUSH
YOU'VE GOT IT! YOU'VE GOT A BABY!
THAT'S IT!
baby? NOT
ALIVE? NOT
wa
waa
yes... HA HA alive
yes... THANK GOD...
alive
haha... then
THEY CLEAN IT ALL UP FOR YOU AND PUT THE LIVER THING IN A BAG AND PUT A LITTLE HAT ON HIM AND IT MAKES YOU
proud
haha...
SO PROUD... OF YOUR WIFE... PROUD..
my
wife
my son...
HA HA
take that, world!...
take that...
BEEP
'grandso

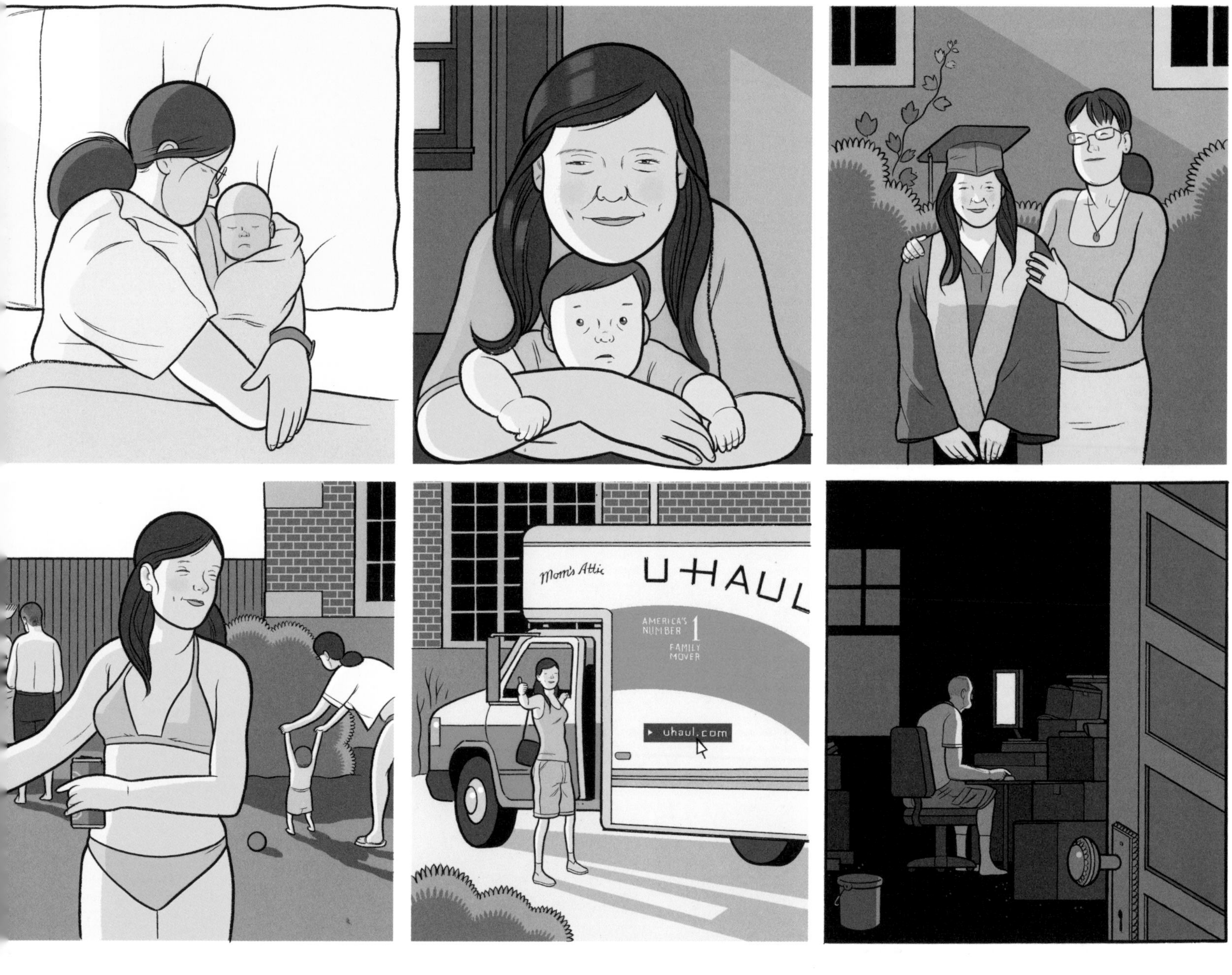

Mom's Attic
U-HAUL
AMERICA'S NUMBER 1 FAMILY MOVER
uhaul.com

OKAY...

I GOT LEVI ASLEEP, BUT...

View Window

View Window
Hide
Full Screen

BUT WHA...

K-KLK

ANOTHER LETTER FROM THE RENTER...

WHICH ONE?

WHICH DO YOU THINK?

:kof:

"DEAR MIZ LINT"

"WE HAVE **AXED** YOU OVER AND OVER TO FIX THE ROOF LEAK AND YOU HADN'T. WE WON'T PAY YOU ANY MORE UNTIL IT IS FIX. OUR LIVING CONDITIONS HERE ARE UN-SAFE TO STAY." AND...

"...AND WE KNOW OUR RIGHTS IN A COURT OF LAW AND WILL EXPRESS THEM TO THE FULLEST EXTEND OF IT."

OKAY FINE...

WE'LL EVICT, THEN...

...WE ALREADY DISCOUNTED THEIR RENT FOR THE ROOF LEAKS, ANYWAY.

DRP

HA HA

GOD

YOU REAL... **ARE** A FUCKING BASTARD AREN'T YO...

Google

abriel lint

Google search | I'm feeling lucky

Results **1 - 10** of **271,321** for **gabriel lint. (0.0004 sec)**

Author Feels Your...
Grueling memoir of life told...
cached - similar

Omaha's Bestselling...
Writer tells grisly tale of...
cached - similar

Show more results in NEWS

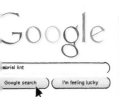

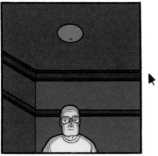

Author Feels Your Pain — and His, Too

New York Times - 59 minutes ago

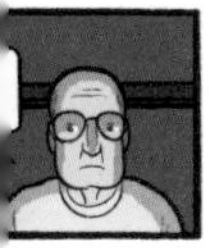

Young memoirist turns a revealing experimental novel of abusive upbringing and self-destructive loneliness into an inspiring literary achievement.

Don't Sweep This Lint Away Washington Post
Bestseller Highlights Role of Parenting FamilyNews

Reuters - Examiner.com - XinHua - CBS2 - Facebook
all 38 news articles >> **email this story**

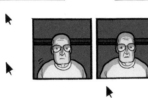

Feelings, Not Words, Tell the Whole Story

By AGNES KONIGSBERG
Published November 29, 2019

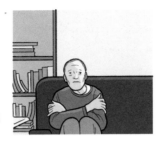

Gabriel Lint

I LOVED YOU
By Gabriel Lint
580 pages. Strathmore Press.
$29 eBook/$59 Paper.

"I've always been a quiet person," says Gabriel Lint, almost inaudibly. "I guess it makes sense that I'm most comfortable in books, or on paper."

Comfortable is hardly a word one would use to describe the slight, headshy 28-year-old, whose bestselling memoir, "I Loved You," has sent him into the spotlight with universally favorable reviews and talk of shortlisting for both the National Book Award and the PEN First Lit prize. "I don't know what to think of it all," says Lint, with a quavering laugh.

Laugh? One might hope to, somewhere, in the midst of this young author's book, but its pages are unrelieved from scenes – or one should really say sensations – of self-laceration, multiple suicide attempts and parental abuse, all rendered in a sometimes disorienting but amazingly discernable language of impressions, phonemes and short bursts of text. One critic has called it "synæsthetic," likening it to Joyce's "revolutionary prose, but in [Mr. Lint's] case one feels as if he's systematically replacing one's memories and feelings with his own." Mr. Lint says more simply, "I guess I just want the reader to feel the things that I did."

Born in Omaha, Nebraska, and raised both there and in Denver, Colorado, Mr. Lint says he always felt out of step with his family and his surroundings. "Back then, especially in the midwest, homosexuality wasn't always something you could discuss. People forget that now. And having deeply religious parents didn't help." Suddenly, his voice fills the Bushwick apartment he's kept since 2017: "I mean, I've forgiven my first Dad. But I don't know why I should." A harrowing account of a broken collarbone opens the book but it's the scene from which the memoir takes its title that has garnered Lint the most glowing praise.

"Early in the story I wanted to depict what it felt like to be in a body that was already losing its will to live, and how an alcoholic personality feeds on that desperation," he says, adding, "particularly since I knew later I'd be depicting my own body as it was losing life itself." Such statements are common for Mr. Lint, who at age 17 left home to live in various Denver squats. He took drugs and played in bands. At the same time he was reading voraciously and keeping a journal. "It was stupid of me, I guess. I was eating out of dumpsters, but I couldn't stop reading and at the same time writing down all of these awful things that'd happened to me."

RECOMMEND
TWITTER
MAIL
SEND TO PHONE
PRINT
SHARE

1 | 2 | 3 NEXT PAGE

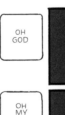

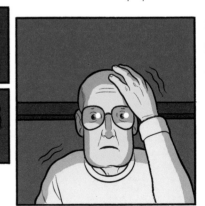

OH GOD
OH MY GOD

BUY "I Loved You" from amazon.com
JOIN "I Loved You" discussion group
READ excerpt of "I Loved You"

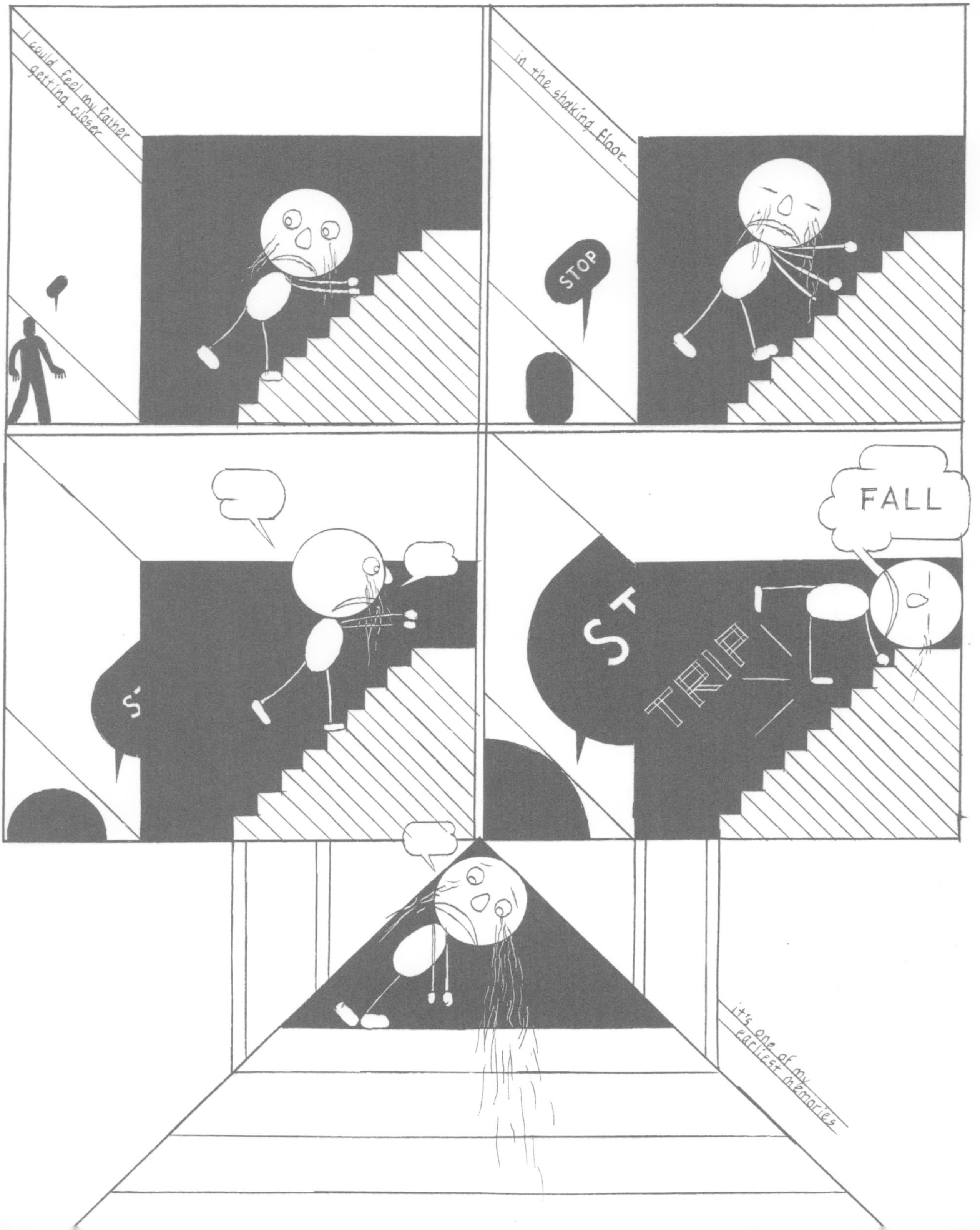

I could feel my father getting closer
in the shaking floor
STOP
S'
ST
FALL
TRIP
it's one of my earliest memories

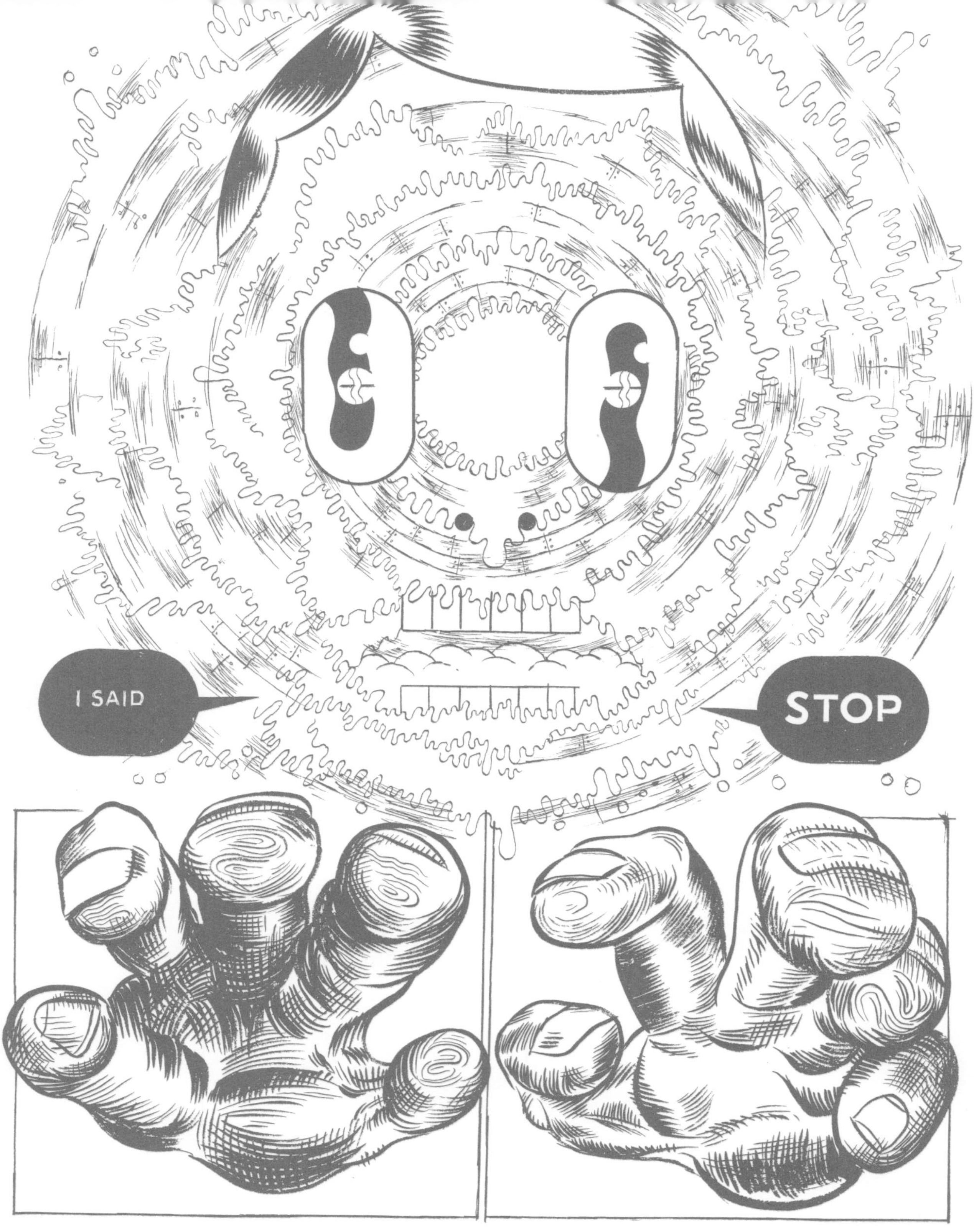
I SAID
STOP

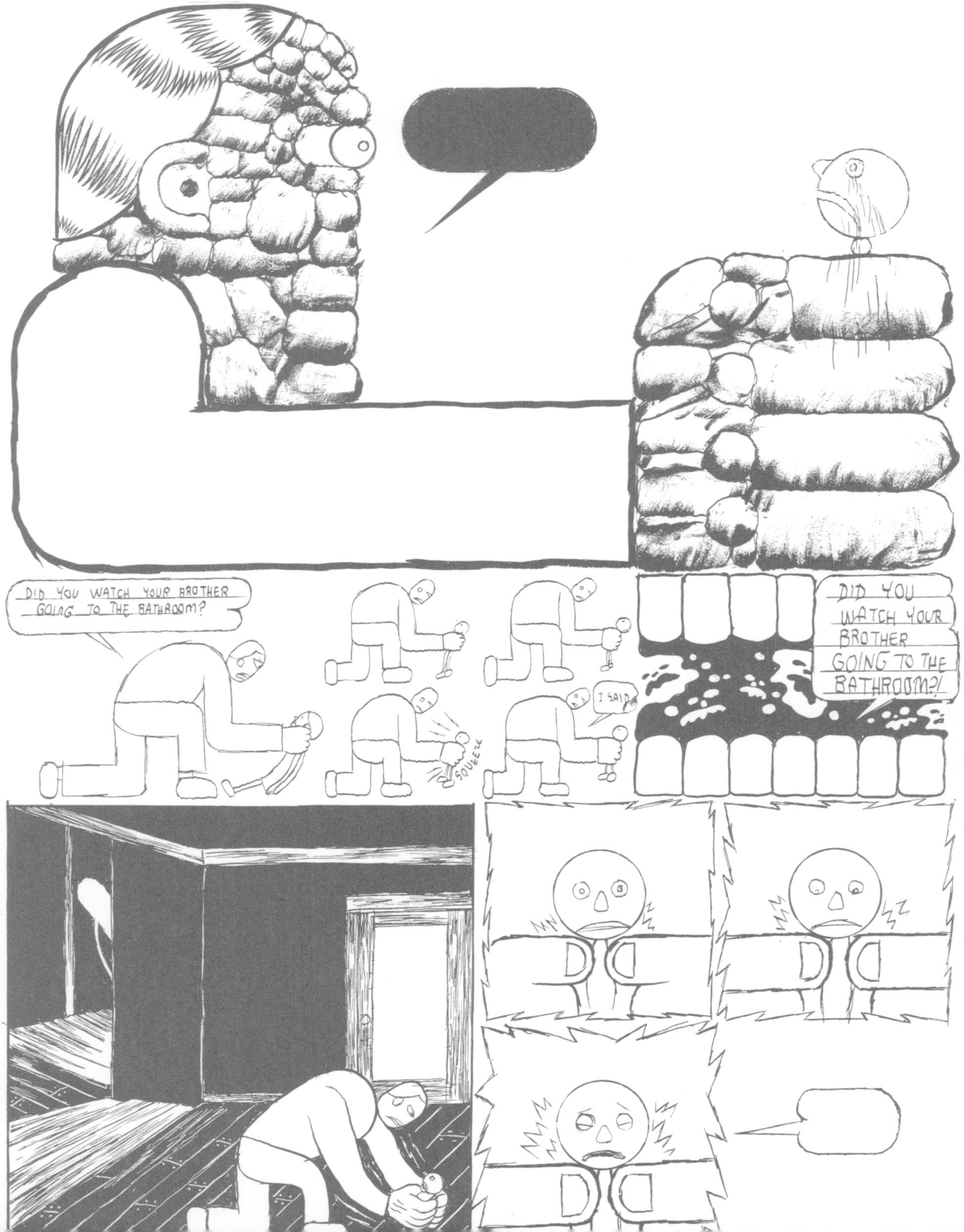
DID YOU WATCH YOUR BROTHER GOING TO THE BATHROOM?
SQUEEZE
I SAID
DID YOU WATCH YOUR BROTHER GOING TO THE BATHROOM?!

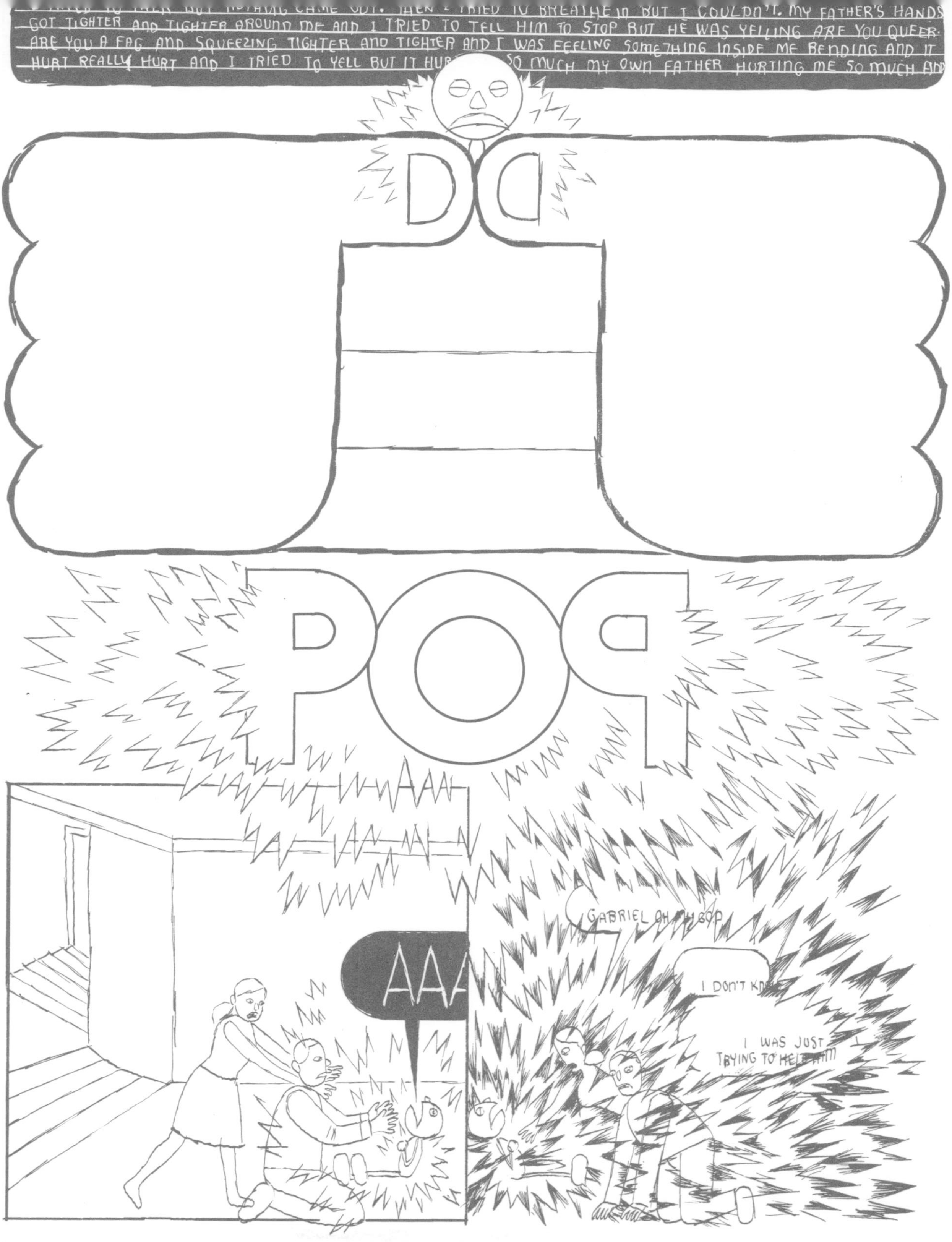
BREATHE IN BUT I COULDN'T. MY FATHER'S HANDS
GOT TIGHTER AND TIGHTER AROUND ME AND I TRIED TO TELL HIM TO STOP BUT HE WAS YELLING ARE YOU QUEER-
ARE YOU A FAG AND SQUEEZING TIGHTER AND TIGHTER AND I WAS FEELING SOMETHING INSIDE ME BENDING AND IT
HURT REALLY HURT AND I TRIED TO YELL BUT IT HUR
SO MUCH MY OWN FATHER HURTING ME SO MUCH AND
POP
AAA
AAA
GABRIEL OH
I DON'T KN
I WAS JUST
TRYING TO HEL

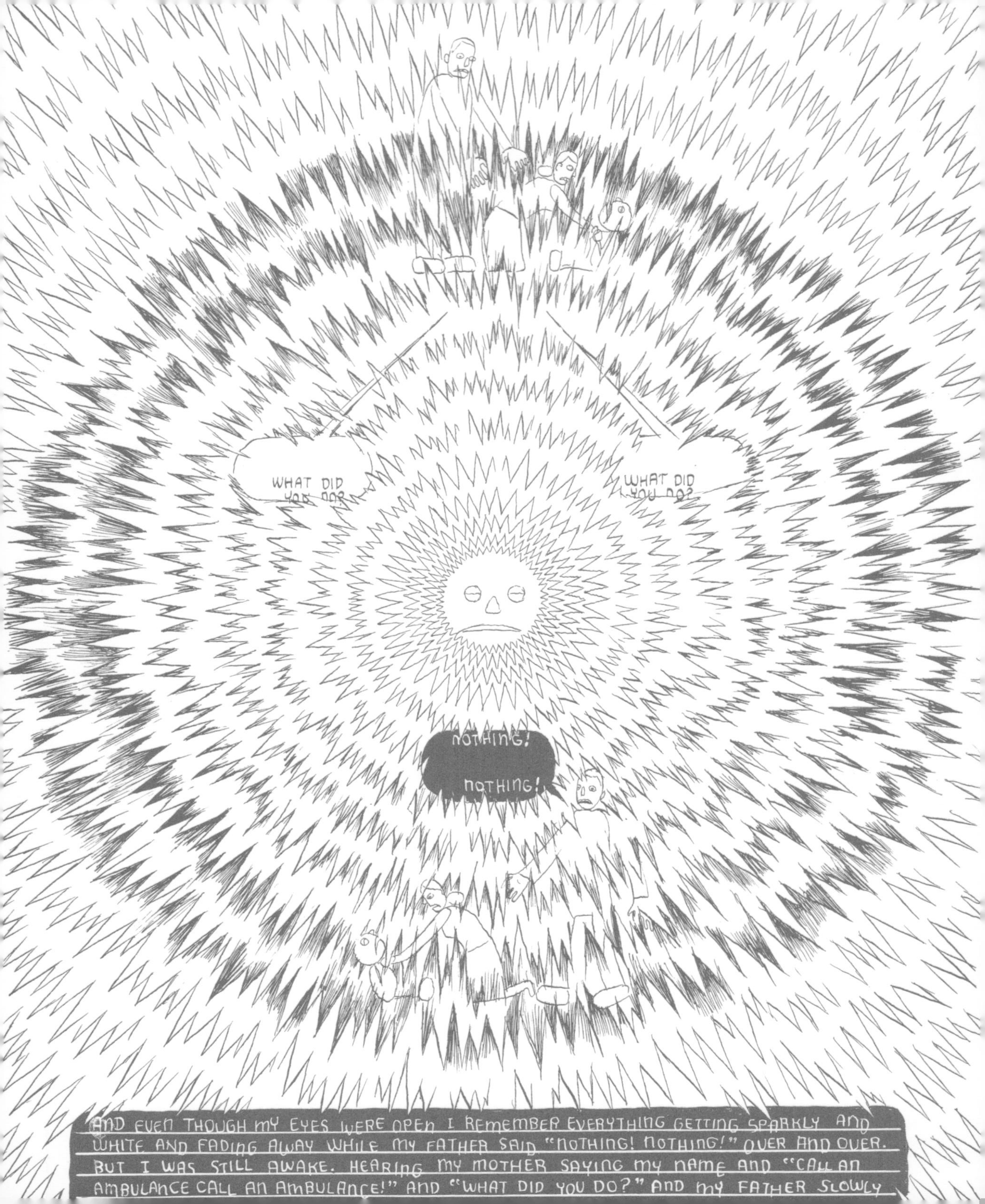
WHAT DID YOU DO?
WHAT DID YOU DO?
NOTHING! NOTHING!
AND EVEN THOUGH MY EYES WERE OPEN I REMEMBER EVERYTHING GETTING SPARKLY AND WHITE AND FADING AWAY WHILE MY FATHER SAID "NOTHING! NOTHING!" OVER AND OVER. BUT I WAS STILL AWAKE. HEARING MY MOTHER SAYING MY NAME AND "CALL AN AMBULANCE CALL AN AMBULANCE!" AND "WHAT DID YOU DO?" AND MY FATHER SLOWLY

an ambulance
did you do?" and
down the stairs,
kind of monster.

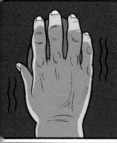

an ambulance
did you do?" and
down the stairs,
kind of monster.

POPPA?

POPPA

POPPA
WHERE'S
MOMMA?

WHERE'S MOMMA,
POPPA?

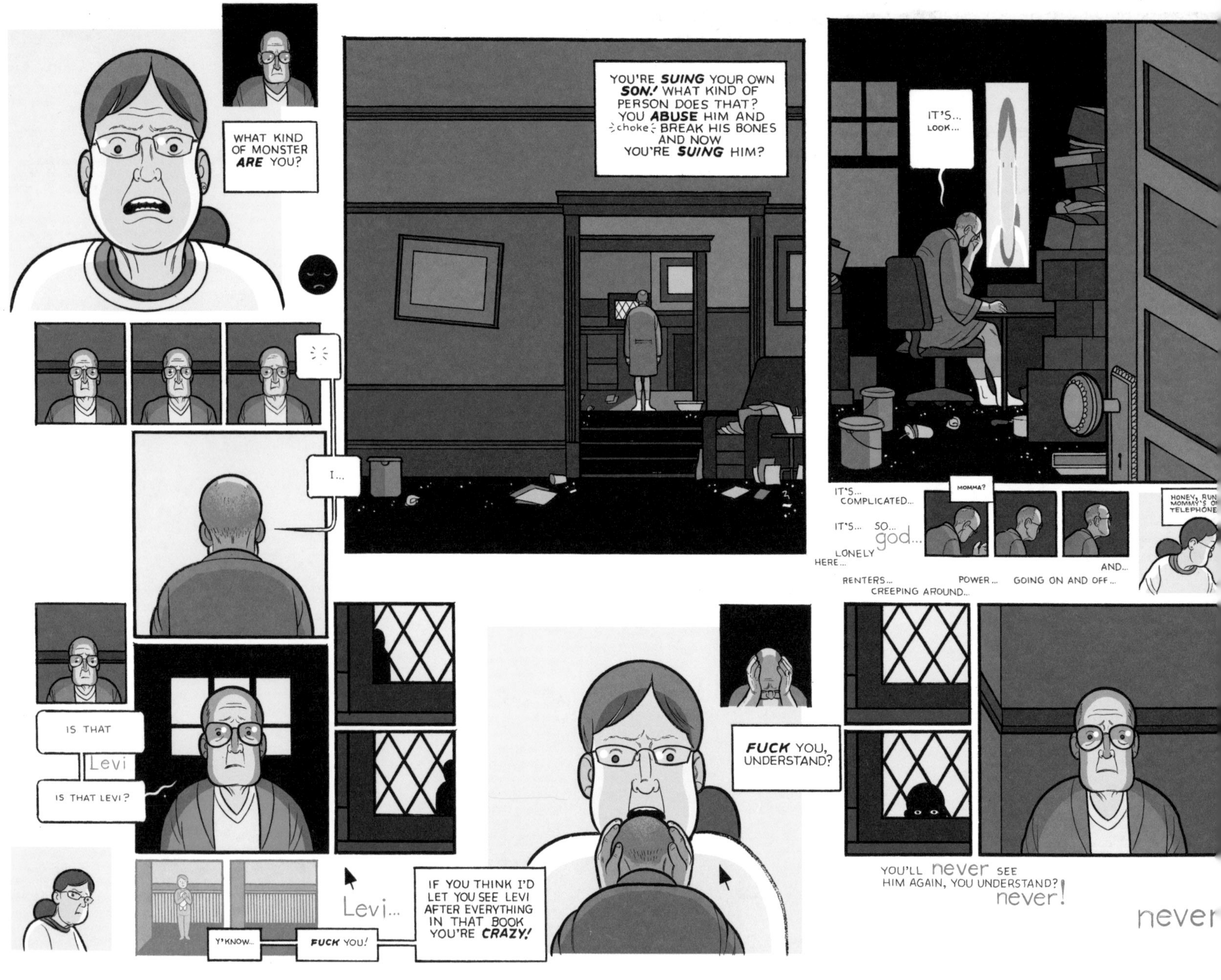

WHAT KIND OF MONSTER **ARE** YOU?
YOU'RE **SUING** YOUR OWN **SON!** WHAT KIND OF PERSON DOES THAT? YOU **ABUSE** HIM AND choke BREAK HIS BONES AND NOW YOU'RE **SUING** HIM?
IT'S... LOOK...
I...
IT'S... COMPLICATED...
IT'S... SO... god...
LONELY HERE...
RENTERS... CREEPING AROUND...
POWER... GOING ON AND OFF... AND...
MOMMA?
HONEY, RUN MOMMY'S ON TELEPHONE
IS THAT
Levi
IS THAT LEVI?
Levi...
Y'KNOW...
FUCK YOU!
IF YOU THINK I'D LET YOU SEE LEVI AFTER EVERYTHING IN THAT BOOK YOU'RE **CRAZY!**
FUCK YOU, UNDERSTAND?
YOU'LL never SEE HIM AGAIN, YOU UNDERSTAND? never!
never

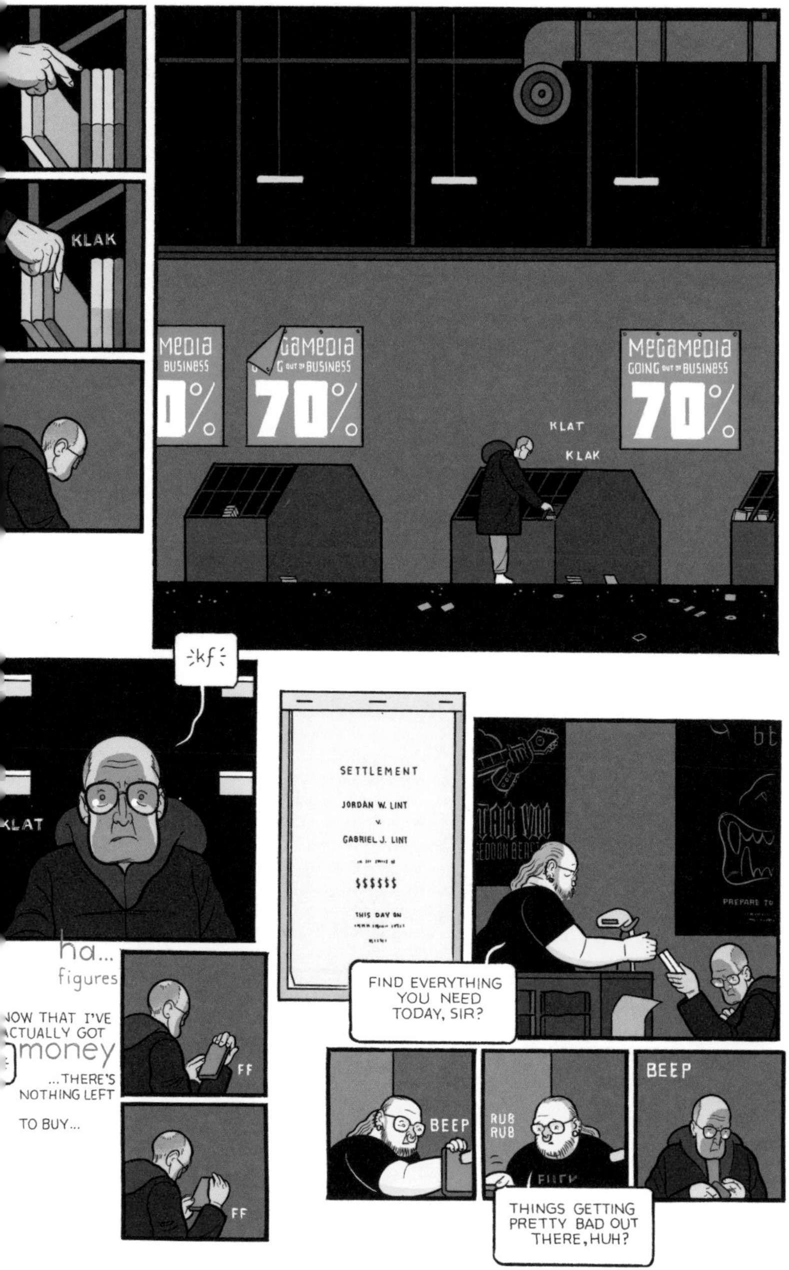
KLAK
Media
BUSINESS
0%
GaMedia
GOING OUT OF BUSINESS
70%
MEGAMEDIA
GOING OUT OF BUSINESS
70%
KLAT
KLAK
kf
KLAT
ha...
figures
OW THAT I'VE
CTUALLY GOT
money
...THERE'S
NOTHING LEFT
TO BUY...
FF
FF
SETTLEMENT
JORDAN W. LINT
v.
GABRIEL J. LINT
$$$$$$
THIS DAY ON
FIND EVERYTHING YOU NEED TODAY, SIR?
BEEP
RUB RUB
BEEP
THINGS GETTING PRETTY BAD OUT THERE, HUH?

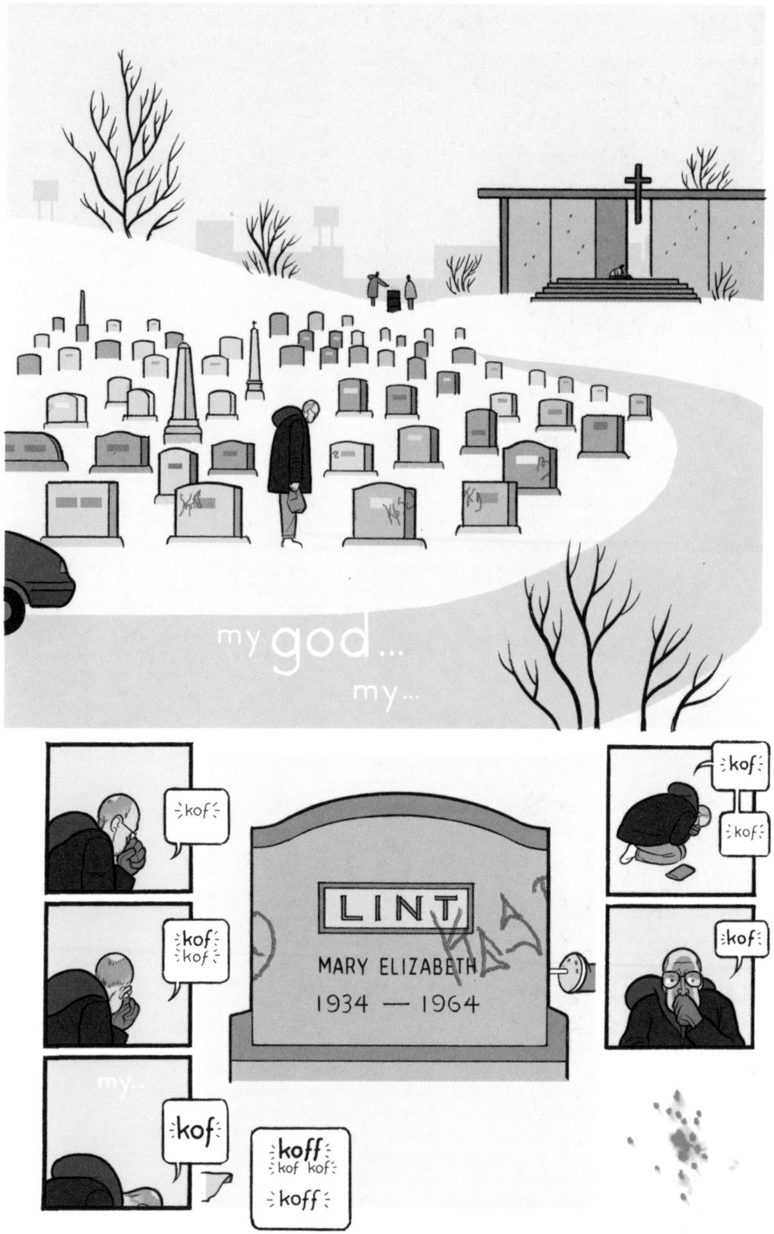
my god...
my...
kof
kof kof
my...
kof
koff kof kof koff
LINT
MARY ELIZABETH
1934 — 1964
kof
kof
kof

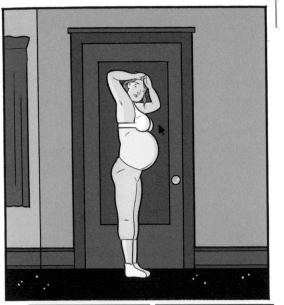

I didn't mean... TO EVER BE SO mean... god... BELIEVE...

YOU'RE THE ONLY ONE ... THE ONLY ONE WHO ...

WHO

WHO IS

oh I'm god... I'm so...

WHO

SHE'S... SHE'S SO...

OH GOD

SHE MAKES ME SO

oh

OH MY POOR SWEETIE

I... I...

I can't believe... ⸝choke⸜

I can't believe...

YOU'D FORGIVE ME... ⸝sob⸜

DON'T CRY...

DON'T CRY...

⸝snf⸜

Y'KNOW,

oh   KRK

I didn't...

⸝huf⸜

FF

⸝huf⸜

⸝huf⸜

KREK

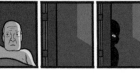

YOU MEAN...

...YOU MEAN YOU'VE BEEN HERE ALL *ALONG?*

WELL *THAT...*

that CHANGES everything

YOU CAN'T... YOU CAN'T... **wow...** imagine how... happy...

hey! hey...

HEY, ARE YOU STILL playing?

Y'KNOW, guitar?

oh **WOW** oh wow I knew it I knew it

LISTEN...

listen... WE'VE GOTTA record, man!

I'VE GOTTA WHOLE SETUP... SOFTWARE, EFFECTS...

god... THAT WOULD BE SO FUCKING cool! wouldn't it?

AND I'VE BEEN WRITING **SONGS**, TOO... ABOUT MY DREAMS...

because

I'VE BEEN HAVING THE MOST amazing... DREAMS, Y'KNOW?

LIKE THE OTHER NIGHT I DREAMED I FOUND THIS LIKE, hidden room YOU KNOW?

AND I realized... that's WHERE ALL THIS water's leaking in BEEN FROM all these years...

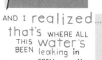

what? GO... what wait!

st**op**!

DON'T ARREST ME! DON'T ARREST ME! I DIDN'T KILL HIM! CAN'T YOU he's alive see? he's alive!!

THEY KEEP MOVING ME, YOU KNOW...

THEY COME IN THE MIDDLE OF THE night BLACK PEOPLE AND THEY move me THE BLACK PEOPLE under the drips AND

MISTER LINT!

MISTER LINT CAN YOU HEAR ME?

HIS CAR'S TEAC DECK

ARRESTED

ARREST HIM

¿huf?

¿huf?

¿huf?

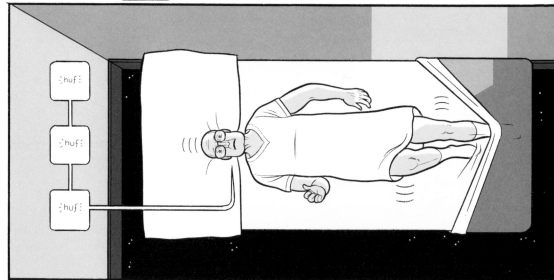

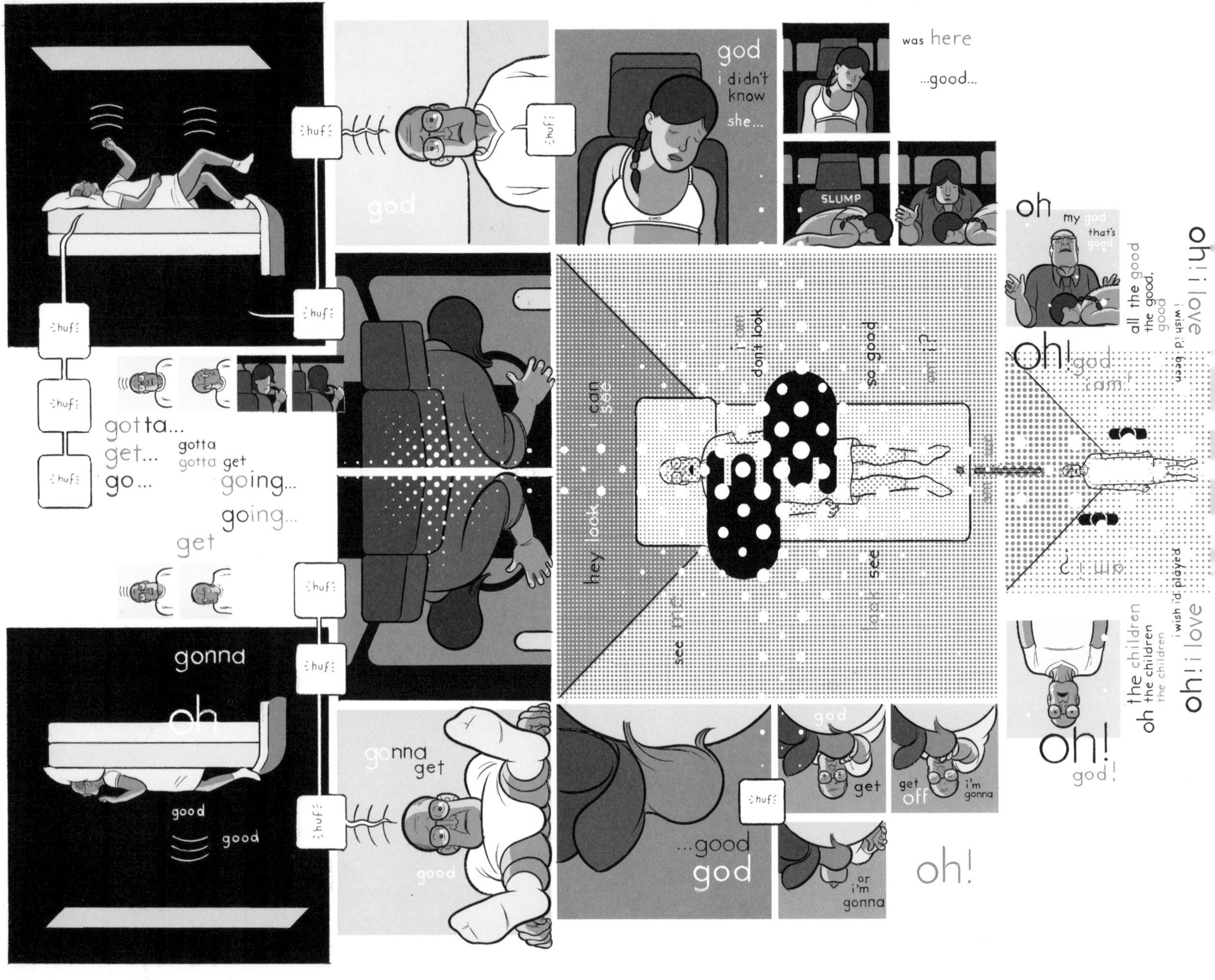

huf
huf
god
god
i didn't
know
she...
was here
...good...
SLUMP
oh
my god
that's
good
oh! i love
all the good
the good,
good
i wish i'd been
oh! god
i am!
i can
see
i
i don't look
so good
am i?
hey look
see me
look see
am i?
i wish i'd played
oh! i love
the children
oh the children
the children
Oh!
god!
gotta...
get...
go...
gotta
gotta get
going...
going...
get
gonna
oh
good
good
gonna
get
good
...good
god
god
get
get
off
i'm
gonna
or
i'm
gonna
oh!